HOW TO GUIDE
GIRL SCOUT DAISIES THROUGH

BETWEEN EARTH AND SKY

IT'S YOUR PLANET—LOVE IT! A LEADERSHIP JOURNEY

A Girl Scout leadership journey invites girls to explore a theme
through many experiences and from many perspectives.
All the joys of travel are built right in: meeting new people, trying new things,
making memories, gathering keepsakes. This guide is your suitcase.
It's packed with everything you need for a wonderful trip that will change girls' lives.

Girl Scouts of the USA

Girl Scouts.

Page 39 and 58: Science process skills and plant part feast details from Katie L. Villano and Christine P. Villano, *WEED WACKERS! K-6 Educators Guide to Invasive Plants of Alaska*, 2008, an independent publication in cooperation with the Alaska Committee for Noxious and Invasive Plant Management, Fairbanks, Alaska.

WRITTEN BY Laura J. Tuchman

CONTRIBUTORS: Toi James, Andrea Bastiani Archibald, Kate Gottlieb, Jennifer Peter

ILLUSTRATED BY Susan Swan

DESIGNED BY Alexander Isley Inc.

MANAGER, OPERATIONS: Sharon Kaplan

GSUSA DESIGN TEAM: Sarah Micklem, Rocco Alberico

© 2009 by Girl Scouts of the USA

First published in 2009 by Girl Scouts of the USA
420 Fifth Avenue, New York, NY 10018-2798
www.girlscouts.org

ISBN: 978-0-88441-737-8

Printed in Italy 7256

2 3 4 5 6 7 8 9/17 16 15 14 13 12 11 10 09

Text printed on Fedrigoni Cento 40 percent de-inked, post-consumer fibers and 60 percent secondary recycled fibers.

Covers printed on Prisma artboard FSC Certified mixed sources.

Mixed Sources
Product group from well-managed forests, controlled sources and recycled wood or fibre
www.fsc.org   Cert no. SGS-COC-004313
©1996 Forest Stewardship Council
FSC

CONTENTS

"One of the main reasons people travel
is because they are hungry
for the authentic and the unique."

— Laura Morelli, *National Geographic Traveler*, March 2008

Flower Friends, and Daisies, on the Road

Girl Scouting has always been about wider opportunities—journeys, both personal and collective, that strengthen girls' values, character, and sense of self.

This leadership journey features the story of three flower friends on a road trip that takes them through some of the world's greatest landscapes. Why that uniqueness is important—why it matters so much to the health of Planet Earth—is the big theme of *Between Earth and Sky*.

The story's scenes and conversations are meant to touch the heart and spark the imagination—not only of the Girl Scout Daisies in your group but of you and your sister volunteers. They are designed to develop a lasting love and respect for the natural world.

It has been said that if you can tell a story about something, you can identify with it. And when you identify with something, you grow to love it. And what you love, you naturally protect.

So it is with this Daisy story, this journey, and the great outdoors of Planet Earth.

Why a Road Trip?

Holiday trips, summer vacations, weekend outings, afternoon excursions—all of these are common occasions for road trips. Before gas prices soared, a cross-country trip was, for some, an annual summer event. That quintessential American travel experience is the inspiration for this Daisy journey.

As any veteran road tripper knows, not all landscapes are created equal. Each road trip has its destination, and the points along the way chosen for rest and refueling are often an uneven mix of timing and desire. Some planned stops fall by the wayside, and new unplanned ones quickly take their place.

In a country as geographically diverse as the United States, some landscapes are so compelling that even young backseat travelers can persuade an adult driver to stop and smell the roses from time to time. But equal time can't be given to everything whizzing by the car windows. As many seasoned travelers like to say, you have to leave something to see on your next visit!

It's in this spirit that Lupe, Clover, and Zinni dive deep in some locations and cruise right by others. Even though they can't stop to enjoy each state's beauty and richness, where they do stop adds up to a memorable vacation. As you and your group of girls journey with them, detour as often as you can to explore the natural attractions of your own region. You'll find tips and suggestions sprinkled through the journey's sample sessions.

Daisies and Everyday Math and Science

As the Daisies explore the natural world around them, you and they will see that science, technology, engineering, and math are as much a part of daily life as food and play.

Yet a troublesome gap often develops between girls' interest and ability in math and science and their desire and confidence to pursue higher education, and ultimately careers, in these fields. To sustain interest and build confidence, Girl Scouts believes that early exposure to the joys and wonders of math and science is crucial—as is encouragement from families, teachers, and the media that is so much a part of daily life.

ENCOURAGING SCIENTIFIC MINDS

Many opportunities to use the basic science skills of observation, communication, and classification are built right into the fun of this journey. So the girls gain a grounding in the foundation of science all along the way.

Between Earth and Sky also introduces girls to many wonders of nature: oceans, lakes, beaches, mountains, deserts, rolling plains. Experiencing this diverse terrain, with all its shapes and colors, furthers the Daisies' natural interests in math and science.

The journey also underscores how essential the sciences and math are to any desire to protect Planet Earth. The girls' book includes short profiles of a variety of women who work to protect and nurture the environment. These women run the gamut from ecologists and biologists to a scientist-artist, a chef, and a basic concerned citizen—someone who could live right next door to you. Make use of these women as role models for the girls, and take advantage of every science and math moment along the journey.

MAKE THE MOST OF EVERY SCIENCE AND MATH MOMENT

- Let Lupe's petal-power car inspire budding engineers and designers.

- Let the journey's travel theme point the way to basic map-reading skills and an introduction to the use of a compass.

- And when the girls count out supplies for a project or count to 10 for hide-and-seek—that's using math without even thinking about it!

The Flower Friends, Storytelling, and Leadership Skills

LOVE AND WONDER

Between Earth and Sky is part of a series of Girl Scout leadership journeys that invites girls, and their families and adult volunteers, to act for the betterment of Earth. The umbrella theme for the series, *It's Your Planet— Love It!*, came directly from a brainstorm with teen Girl Scouts. Its sentiment is at the core of the road trip story.

By the end of the journey, the Daisies will see that travel is about far more than just getting from here to there. It's an adventure that opens their eyes to new experiences, and all the wonders of the world.

In "A Road Trip to Remember," the story at the heart of this journey, several flower friends head to Alaska to check in on a cousin named White Sweetclover. Each session of the journey features a section of the road trip story, so a Story Time—a reading and discussion period—is built into each gathering you have with the girls.

Activities in each sample session also build on the story's themes to teach girls valuable leadership skills and values: critical thinking, conflict resolution, building healthy relationships, identifying community needs, advocacy, and feeling empowered to make a difference in the world. These skills and values are the building blocks of the Girl Scout Leadership Experience—and they all rely on good communication. So it's no wonder that the flower friends are such great talkers. They communicate with one another, share feelings and hopes, and reach beyond their circle to make the world a better place.

To develop their own communication skills, Daisies take part in role-playing activities that parallel the story's action. For example, as the flowers get ready for their trip, with Zinni wanting to help Lupe, the Daisies consider how they might help a friend, and they talk about where and why they like to travel.

Role-playing teaches Daisies the values of the Girl Scout Law, and gives them opportunities to learn about themselves and the wide world around them—all while moving them toward national Girl Scout leadership outcomes.

ONE STORY, MANY OPTIONS

Given the richness of the road trip story, each journey session offers a variety of options to explore. Depending on the time available and the girls' interest, you might pursue some of these in greater depth, perhaps even expanding a few into multiple sessions. The journey can then be enjoyed over a much longer period than the 10 sample sessions provided in this guide.

IMAGINATION AND LOVE OF LANGUAGE

Besides inspiring real-life action, stories spark the imagination and build a love and appreciation of language. So consider lining up "guest readers"—teen or adult—to add flair to each Story Time and really bring the flowers' road trip alive for the Daisies. Fun vocabulary pointers, called Words for the Wise, are built into the girls' book, and the sample sessions offer opportunities for the girls to learn new words that match up with the leadership skills they are building.

TEACHABLE MOMENTS ON THE ROAD

The road trip story also offers many "teachable moments." Some are obvious, such as Zinni wanting to help Lupe get ready to travel, or Sunny cleaning soil in Pittsburgh. Others, such as how sleepy Lupe gets after eating a lot of cheese and drinking a lot of milk, will call for a bit of explanation on your part—but not much! And they'll all leave the Daisies that much wiser.

Use the story's teachable moments to point out important lessons to the girls, particularly those related to health and well-being and leadership. For example, use the flowers taking a float in the Great Salt Lake to point out the difference between a fairy tale with talking flowers who enjoy some time in saltwater (though do note that the flowers are careful to keep their heads and their roots above the water!) and the real world, where flowers need fresh water and dunking them in strongly salted water is a usually a no-no.

Other teachable moments are more subtle and will depend on your region and how its assets (trees, birds, scientists, and other community members) match up with the road trip story. Have fun guiding the girls through these moments when you happen upon ones that interest you and the Daisies.

Snapshot of the Journey

SESSION 1

Getting Ready
for the Road

The Daisies begin to express their feelings and start to understand and experience the joys of travel, especially outdoors in nature.

SESSION 2

The Road Trip
Begins

The Daisies continue to explore what makes them unique as they start to consider the feelings of their sister Daisies and expand their knowledge of shapes in nature.

SESSION 3

You, Me,
How Different
We Can Be

The Daisies continue to explore their feelings and how they might differ from one girl to another. They also explore the range of colors in nature and earn their Blue Bucket Award.

SESSION 4

Living the Law,
and So Many
Seeds

The Daisies explore living the Girl Scout Law through favorite flower friends and expand their knowledge of seeds and how they travel as a step to understanding how vegetation can vary around the world. The girls also try their hand at origami.

SESSION 5

Special Skills,
and Textures, Too

The Daisies continue to explore their similarities and differences as they consider the skills they contribute to their Daisy group and gain an understanding of the diversity of shapes in nature.

SESSION 6

We Have Skills and So Do Plants

The Daisies make use of their special skills and begin to understand the special skills of plants, too. The girls also have an option to paint with natural colors made from fruits, vegetables, and other natural items, and they earn their Firefly Award.

SESSION 7

In the Land of Milk and Cheese

The girls take the flowers friends story to a personal level by learning about how foods can affect how they feel and by tasting foods from their region. They also take a walk in nature to explore textures.

SESSION 8

When the Flowers Meet the Trees

The Daisies choose a project idea, practice talking about it, and create visual tools for their project. They also have an option to make bark rubbings.

SESSION 9

Protecting a Natural Treasure

The Daisies team up to protect a natural treasure of Earth and hear the final chapter of the flower friends' road trip story.

SESSION 10

On the Road to New Adventures

The Daisies celebrate all they've learned and done along the journey! The girls also earn the Clover Award.

Flower Friends, Global Themes

In "A Road Trip to Remember," the flower friends make stops at various places throughout the United States. They see cities, woodlands, rolling farmland, desert, beaches, a lake, and oceans. If the girls already enjoyed *Welcome to the Daisy Flower Garden*, they may remember that the flowers come from various parts of the country and have family all around the world.

Lupe, the lupine is blue and honest and fair. She loves to summer in Maine. She's in the driver's seat on this journey's road trip.

Zinni, the zinnia, is spring green. She's considerate and caring. She's from Mexico and is Lupe's first passenger on the trip.

Gloria, the morning glory, is purple. She represents the Girl Scout Law line, "respect myself and others." She hosts her flower friends at her inn in Maine.

Sunny, the sunflower, is from Great Britain and is friendly and helpful. She joins the road trip in Pittsburgh.

Clover is green and sports white flowers. She uses resources wisely. She and her cousins join the road trip, too—to get to Alaska.

This makes them a great springboard for exploring various cultures. You might invite teens or adults who grew up in regions other than your own to join a Daisy gathering to talk about their hometowns, and the foods and trees that grow there. Guide the Daisies to see that differences are what make people—and places and plants—unique and interesting, and that differences, as well as similarities, are to be respected and appreciated.

Daisy represents all parts of the Girl Scout Law. The Daisy Flower Garden is named for her—and for all Girl Scout Daisies, including Girl Scouts founder Juliette "Daisy" Gordon Low.

Tula, the tulip, is red and courageous and strong. She's from Holland. She meets up with her traveling friends in Washington State.

Gerri, the geranium, is magenta and respects authority. She stays home in the Daisy Flower Garden.

Rosie, the rose, likes to "make the world a better place." She joins the road trip in California.

Mari, the marigold, is orange and "responsible for what I say and do." She stays home in the Daisy Flower Garden.

Vi, the violet, is "a sister to every Girl Scout." She's from Australia. She stays in the Daisy garden, too.

Awards Along the Journey

Daisies have the opportunity to earn three prestigious leadership awards as they seek new challenges on this *Between Earth and Sky* journey. The steps to the awards, which are woven directly into the Sample Sessions, have the girls consider their feelings and skills and then take into account the feelings and skills of those around them. The girls then move on to engage their larger community. You might think of the Daisies' award steps as a series of collections: First they collect words and deeds—ways of talking and acting. Then they collect useful skills and ways of doing. And then they move out into their community to "do."

You might spark the excitement of this award series by presenting the *Between Earth and Sky* background patch to all the Daisies at their first session. Or choose another time. There's no set way to present it. You might even pass it out at a Daisy Friends and Family gathering that you hold before the journey starts.

Here are the three awards and the steps the Daisies will take to earn them:

A BUCKET FOR WORDS

The Blue Bucket Award is named for the blue bucket seats of flower friend Lupe's petal-power car. Just as Lupe and her friends get what they need from their bucket seats, the real Daisies dip into their bucket for leadership words that help them tackle an array of situations.

The Blue Bucket Award

This first award encourages girls to become aware of their feelings and the feelings of those around them. It also encourages them to develop good relationship skills: for negotiating and compromising to resolve conflicts, and for being considerate and caring to others.

To earn the award, the girls:

- tell one another about their feelings and the feelings of those around them.
- take part in role-playing activities that encourage them to resolve conflicts, negotiate, and be considerate to others.

The steps to this award are built into the suggested activities in Sample Sessions 1, 2, and 3. A good time for girls to earn the award is at the end of Session 3.

The Firefly Award

This second award is earned as the Daisies recognize and develop their skills and then choose a skill they will educate and inspire others about. By making an effort that moves beyond themselves, the girls begin to realize the impact that they can have on others around them.

To earn the award, the girls:

- Think about and talk about their own skills and those of their sister Daisies.

- Choose a skill that they can teach others, either at home or in their community.

- Steps to this award are built into the suggested activities in Sample Sessions 4, 5, and 6. A good time for the girls to earn this award is at the end of Session 6.

The Clover Award

Girls earn this third award as they team up to protect a natural treasure in their region. The award is named for flower friend Clover, who helps preserve the natural habitat of Alaska by convincing her cousin White Sweetclover to leave the state so that its natural vegetation can flourish.

To earn the award, the girls:

- learn about and commit to protecting a natural treasure in their region.

- educate and inspire others in their community to join with them to protect the local treasure, too.

(Suggestions for Clover projects are on pages 82–83.) Girls plan and carry out their project throughout Sessions 7–9. A good time for the girls to earn the award is at the journey's closing celebration.

Health, Safety, and Well-Being

The emotional and physical safety and well-being of girls is of paramount importance in Girl Scouting. Look out for the safety of girls by following the Girl Scout Activity Checkpoints when planning all gatherings and trips, and:

- Check into any additional safety guidelines your council might provide.
- Talk to girls and their families about special needs or concerns.

Welcoming Girls with Disabilities

Girl Scouting embraces girls with many different needs and is guided by a very specific and positive philosophy of inclusion that benefits all: Each girl is an equal and valued member of a group with typically developing peers.

As an adult volunteer, you have the chance to improve the way society views girls with disabilities. One way to start is with language. Your words have a huge impact on the process of inclusion. People-First Language puts the person before the disability:

SAY	INSTEAD OF
She has autism.	She's autistic.
She has an intellectual disability.	She's mentally retarded.
She has a learning disability.	The girl is learning-disabled.
She uses a wheelchair.	She is wheelchair-bound.
She has a disability.	She is handicapped.

LEARN WHAT A GIRL NEEDS

First, don't assume that because a person has a disability, she needs assistance or special accommodations. Probably the most important thing you can do is to ask the individual girl or her parents or guardians what she needs to make her experience in Girl Scouts successful. If you are frank with the girl and her parents and make yourself accessible to them, it's likely they will respond in kind, creating a better experience for all.

It's important for all girls to be rewarded based on their best efforts—not on completion of a task. Give any girl the opportunity to do her best and she will. Sometimes that means changing a few rules or approaching an activity in a more creative way. Here are a few examples:

- Invite a girl to perform an activity after observing others doing it first.

- Ask the girls to come up with ideas on how to adapt an activity.

- Often what counts most is staying flexible and varying your approach. For a list of resources, visit www.girlscouts.org and search on "disability resources."

Snacking Smart Along *Between Earth and Sky!*

If the Daisies meet after school, they'll likely need a snack. Encourage members of your Daisy Friends and Family Network to take turns providing them. Earthy treats, like vegetables and fruits, will be fun for the journey—and are generally healthful, too. Ideas for festive snacks are offered throughout the sessions and page 92 of the girls' book features one, too. Consider asking your Network to bring:

- sliced fruits and vegetables, especially those with bright colors

- locally produced foods, such as cheeses, breads, or any items unique to your region

Be sure to check in with Daisy families about any food allergies.

GIRL SCOUT COUNCIL CONTACT INFO
Name: _____
_____
_____
Can help with: _____
_____
_____
Phone: _____
E-mail: _____

The Girl Scout Promise and Law

If the girls are first-year Daisies, let them know early on about a very important part of Girl Scouting: the Girl Scout Promise. A good way to do this is to gather the girls in a Daisy Circle and explain that they now have something special, which is shared by all Girl Scouts: the Girl Scout Promise.

Explain that the Promise (which you have written on a whiteboard/chalkboard or large sheet of paper—recycled is best!) is the way Girl Scouts agree to act toward one another and other people. After you read the full Promise, read it again, line by line, and ask the girls to repeat each line after you.

Once all four lines are said, ask the girls to say the whole Promise again, together with you. Explain to any first-year Daisies that they are starting to know an important part of Girl Scouting. And congratulate any second-year Daisies who already know the Promise. Let all the girls know that they will say the Promise together as a team each time they meet. And let them decide when they'd like to say it. Ask: *Would you like to say the Promise together when we start our Daisy time together or right before we are about to go home?*

Then talk to the girls about the last line of the Promise, which says that the Daisies will try to "live by the Girl Scout Law."

The Girl Scout Promise

On my honor, I will try:
* To serve God and my country,*
* To help people at all times,*
* And to live by the Girl Scout Law.*

Explain that the Girl Scout Law spells out all the good ways that Girl Scouts try to treat one another and the world—being kind and considerate, and friendly and helpful, caring and thoughtful, and so forth.

Explain that the Law is an important part of Girl Scouting that they'll do their best to follow throughout their time as Girl Scouts. Emphasize that they'll learn more about the Law in the story "A Road Trip to Remember," which they will hear parts of at each Daisy gathering. And remind them that they can see the Law on the inside cover of their book, where each line is paired with its flower friend.

SECOND-YEAR DAISIES? NEW GIRLS, TOO?

If the girls in your group are not new to Girl Scouting, invite them say the Promise and Law in their customary way, either at the opening or closing of their gatherings.

If the group is mixed, you might suggest that second-year Daisies take a turn at being friendly and helpful by assisting younger girls in the group. Remind them that being friendly and helpful is a line from the Girl Scout Law—and a key Girl Scout value.

THE GIRL SCOUT PROMISE

On my honor, I will try:
To serve God and my country,
To help people at all times,
And to live by the Girl Scout Law.

THE GIRL SCOUT LAW

I will do my best to be

honest and fair,

friendly and helpful,

considerate and caring,

courageous and strong, and

responsible for what I say and do,

and to

respect myself and others,

respect authority,

use resources wisely,

make the world a better place, and

be a sister to every Girl Scout.

Lupe, Zinni, Mari, Sunny, Tula, Gerri, Gloria, Clover, Rosie, Vi

19

Daisies and the Great Outdoors

**TAKE TIME TO
BE CURIOUS!**

"You do not have to be a 'nature expert' to carry on a good nature program. You just need to revive your own childhood curiosity . . . Probably one of the most baffling things in the world to a child is the 'nature' of grown-ups, which seems to them so indifferent to . . . really important things . . . Imagine . . . being too busy to stop and watch the butterfly about to come out of the cocoon, or the cat chase her own tail . . . "

—*Leader's Guide,* 1950

**MAKE OUTINGS
GIRL LED**

Engage the girls in choosing where to go and what to do. And encourage them to brainstorm who they might want to meet on their outings. Park rangers? Naturalists? Scientists? Farmers?

What questions could the Daisies ask these experts that might deepen their appreciation of nature?

Daisy-age girls have plenty to keep them occupied in the great outdoors. Enjoying nature is the foundation for a lasting love and respect for the environment, so consider inviting the Daisies on a range of outdoor excursions:

- **Day trips to local nature areas**, including parks and nature preserves, let girls experience the natural world of their region firsthand.

- **Parks, gardens, natural history museums, and zoos** are among the great urban places for enriching, nature-filled adventures. There's no limit to what the girls can explore in them. They might, for example, check out any plants they see growing. How many are local? How many are exotic and brought in for their pleasing looks? As a group, they might ask a few questions of staff members or other experts they meet.

- **Neighborhood walks** and other brief excursions offer opportunities for the girls to explore nature right in their own backyard. Seeing weeds sprouting amid plants leads to one of the journey's central questions: "Why are some plants good for one area and not good for others?"

BEFORE VENTURING OUTDOORS . . .

Follow the Girl Scout motto: Be prepared! Talk to the Daisies about how to treat plants and animals with care. Start with Leave No Trace principles.

Leave No Trace is a way to enjoy nature without disturbing it. You'll see a few subtle references to it in the girls' book on pages 23 and 96.

Let the Daisies know that to Leave No Trace means they can pick up natural items (leaves, twigs, seeds, nuts) that have fallen to the ground, but they should not pick, pluck, or otherwise disturb living things. That means not disturbing any plants and wildlife, including homes, such as nests or burrows, even those that might appear to be abandoned.

You might also talk with the girls about what "Do Not Disturb" means with plants and animals outdoors in nature. *Would it include:*

- *not flipping over rocks to look underneath?*

- *not pulling up moss?*

- *not ripping leaves from bushes?*

- *not stomping on holes that might house animals or insects?*

What else can the girls think of that should not be disturbed?

NOT YET A NATURE ENTHUSIAST?

Ask your council for training. Or ask to be paired with an experienced volunteer when you venture outdoors with the girls.

ON OUTINGS, SAFETY IN NUMBERS

No matter where you venture, plan on one adult for every six Daisies. Add more support as needed based on the girls' readiness for outdoor adventures and your, and your co-volunteers', level of experience.

SEIZE EVERY MOMENT

If girls spot weeds taking over a garden, or seeds blowing in the wind, turn these moments into opportunities to talk about wise ways to care for nature.

Making the Most of Daisies' Skills

IN MIXED-AGE GROUPS

In groups with both kindergartners and first-graders, skills may vary. So encourage older girls to mentor younger ones.

When planning outdoor adventures, be aware that kindergartners and first-graders:

Need to run, walk, and play outside.	*So, they will enjoy going on nature walks and outdoor scavenger hunts.*
Are concrete thinkers and focused on the here and now.	*So don't just talk about plants and trees. Take the girls outside for real-life examples and experiences for greater understanding.*
Are great builders.	*So they are more than able to build a dam for a small waterway with rocks and stones, or a bird's nest with sticks and twigs.*
Are only beginning to learn about basic number concepts.	*So take opportunities to count out steps with the girls to estimate distance or make measurements.*
Love to move and dance.	*So they might like to move and act like animals in their habitats, or dance like wind, snow, and rain!*
Are beginning to learn how to write and spell.	*So when they are planning or recording outdoor activities, encourage them to do so through drawings in addition to any writing.*
Know how to follow simple directions and respond well to recognition for doing so.	*So be specific and offer only one direction at a time. Acknowledging when the girls have followed the direction well will also increase their motivation for listening and following through again!*

Girl Scout Traditions and Ceremonies

Celebrating Girl Scout traditions connects girls to one another, to their sister Girl Scouts and Girl Guides around the world, and to the generations of girls who were Girl Scouts before them.

Along *Between Earth and Sky*, you'll notice frequent opportunities to gather in Daisy Friendship Circles, and hold award ceremonies. Your Girl Scout council might celebrate other traditions that you can incorporate into the journey, too. Here are a few of the most enduring Girl Scout traditions:

GIRL SCOUT SIGN

The Girl Scout sign is made when you say the Girl Scout Promise. The sign is formed with the right hand, by using the thumb to hold down the little finger, leaving the three middle fingers extended to represent the three parts of the Promise.

QUIET SIGN

The Quiet Sign is a way to silence a crowd without shouting at anyone. The sign is made by holding up the right hand with all five fingers extended. It refers to the original Fifth Law of Girl Scouting: A Girl Scout is courteous.

GIRL SCOUT HANDSHAKE

The Girl Scout handshake is the way many Girl Guides and Girl Scouts greet each other. They shake their left hands while making the Girl Scout sign with their right hand.

FRIENDSHIP CIRCLE

The Friendship Circle is often formed at the end of meetings or campfires as a closing ceremony. Everyone gathers in a circle, and each girl crosses her right arm over her left and holds hands with the person on each side. Once everyone is silent, the leader starts the friendship squeeze by squeezing the hand of the person next to her. One by one, each girl passes on the squeeze until it travels around the full circle.

TRADITIONS, CEREMONIES, AND LEADERSHIP

Traditions and ceremonies have always been part of the fun of being a Girl Scout.

When girls gather in a ceremony, they share their strengths, hopes, and accomplishments, and experience the power of belonging. Traditions really show girls that they're part of a sisterhood of leaders.

So involve the Daisies in creating some new traditions—even silly songs!

LEFT HAND = FRIENDSHIP

The left-handed handshake represents friendship because the left hand is closer to the heart than the right.

What + How: Creating a Quality Experience

It's not just *what* girls do, but *how* you engage them that creates a high-quality experience. All Girl Scout activities are built on three processes that make Girl Scouting unique from school and other extracurricular activities. When used together, these processes—Girl Led, Learning by Doing, and Cooperative Learning—ensure the quality and promote the fun and friendship so integral to Girl Scouting. Take some time to understand these processes and how to use them with Daisies.

Girl Led

"Girl led" is just what it sounds like—girls play an active part in figuring out the what, where, when, how, and why of their activities. So encourage them to lead the planning, decision-making, learning, and fun as much as possible. This ensures that girls are engaged in their learning and experience leadership opportunities as they prepare to become active participants in their local and global communities. With Daisies, you could:

- help girls decide on certain aspects (who, what, where, when, and how) of activities
- identify activities that girls can appropriately take the lead on and notice how confident they are in expressing themselves
- encourage girls to volunteer for projects they think they would be good at

Learning by Doing

Learning by Doing is a hands-on learning process that engages girls in continuous cycles of action and reflection that result in deeper understanding of concepts and mastery of practical skills. As they participate in meaningful activities and then reflect on them, girls get to explore their own questions, discover answers, gain new skills, and share ideas and observations with others.

KEEP IT GIRL LED

From beginning to end, keep your eye on what the girls want to do and the direction they seem to be taking. It's the approach begun by Juliette Gordon Low: When she and her associates couldn't decide on a new direction, she often said, "Let's ask the girls!"

Girl Led experiences are built right into this journey to make it easy for you.

At each session, ask the girls for their own thoughts on what they've done or discussed.

Throughout the process, it's important for girls to be able to connect their experiences to their lives and apply what they have learned to their future experiences both within and outside of Girl Scouting. With Daisies, you could:

- set up opportunities for girls to explore and create with real materials and tools that are safe and age-appropriate

- model learning by doing and demonstrate hands-on activities that require assistance from a girl

- Develop activities that get girls "out of their seat" and involved

Cooperative Learning

Through cooperative learning, girls work together toward shared goals in an atmosphere of respect and collaboration that encourages the sharing of skills, knowledge, and learning. Moreover, given that many girls desire to connect with others, cooperative learning may be a particularly meaningful and enjoyable way to engage girls in learning. Working together in all-girl environments also encourages girls to feel powerful and emotionally and physically safe, and it allows them to experience a sense of belonging even in the most diverse groups. With Daisies, you could:

- give girls examples of what cooperation and collaboration look like

- create activities for girls that must be completed in groups

- promote social skills, such as listening and taking turns

LEARNING BY DOING

The girls have opportunities to reflect on their experiences and apply them to their lives throughout the journey, particularly in the role-play activities built into the sessions.

TEAMWORK, TOO

Throughout the journey, the girls take part in activities that build teamwork and cooperation. Starting in Session 1, the Daisies team up to solve a conflict. Throughout the journey, you might ask each girl to reflect on how her teammates' thoughts, feelings, and actions have helped her see differences in the world.

Understanding the Journey's Leadership Benefits

Filled with fun and friendship, *Between Earth and Sky* is designed to develop the skills and values young girls need to be leaders now and as they grow. The journey's activities are designed to enable Daisies to strive toward achieving 13 of 15 national outcomes, or benefits, of the Girl Scout Leadership Experience, as summarized on the next page.

Each girl is different, so don't expect them all to exhibit the same signs to indicate what they are learning along the journey. What matters is that you are guiding the Daisies toward leadership skills and qualities they can use right now—and all their lives.

For full definitions of the outcomes and the signs that Daisies are achieving them, see the chart on the next page or *Transforming Leadership: Focusing on Outcomes of the New Girl Scout Leadership Experience* (GSUSA, 2008). Keep in mind that the intended benefits to girls are the cumulative result of traveling through an entire journey—and everything else girls experience in Girl Scouting.

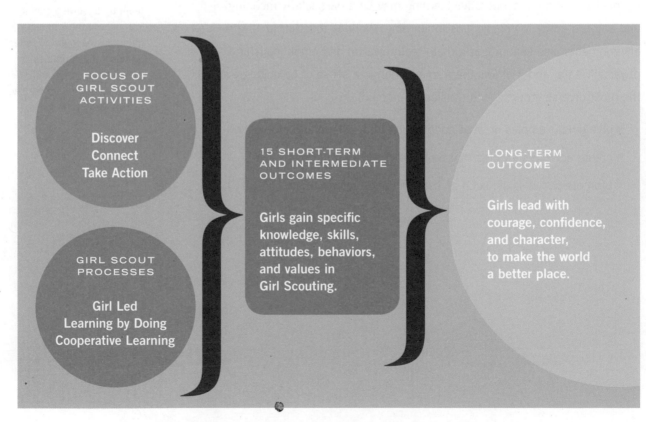

FOCUS OF GIRL SCOUT ACTIVITIES

Discover
Connect
Take Action

GIRL SCOUT PROCESSES

Girl Led
Learning by Doing
Cooperative Learning

15 SHORT-TERM AND INTERMEDIATE OUTCOMES

Girls gain specific knowledge, skills, attitudes, behaviors, and values in Girl Scouting.

LONG-TERM OUTCOME

Girls lead with courage, confidence, and character, to make the world a better place.

NATIONAL LEADERSHIP OUTCOMES

		AT THE DAISY LEVEL, girls . . .	RELATED ACTIVITIES (by Session or girls' book chapter/page)	SAMPLE "SIGN" When the outcome is achieved, girls might . . .
DISCOVER	Girls develop a strong sense of self.	are better able to recognize their strengths and abilities.	S6: Opening Ceremony, Closing Ceremony; GB: When Soon is Better, p. 49	make positive statements about their abilities or demonstrate to others what they can do.
	Girls develop positive values.	begin to understand the values inherent in the Girl Scout Promise and Law.	S3: Story Time; S4: Opening and Closing; S10: Opening Ceremony; GB: pp. 10, 14, 20, 22, 23, 62, and 77; all women and girl profiles; Chapter 6	identify actions that are fair/unfair, honest/dishonest in various scenarios.
		recognize that their choices of actions or words have an effect on others and the environment.	S7, S8, S9: Clover Project; GB: pp. 13–14, 42–46, 50, 58, 69, 84, and 96; Chapter 6	give an example of when their actions made something better for someone else.
	Girls gain practical life skills—girls practice healthy living.	gain greater knowledge of what is healthy for mind and body.	S3: Feast of Plant Parts; S4: Story Time; S7: Story Time; S8: Snack Time; GB: pp. 53, 65, and 93	name behaviors that contribute to good health (e.g., eating fruit, getting exercise).
	Girls seek challenges in the world.	demonstrate increased interest in learning new skills.	All nature, science, art activities; S2–S6: Opening, Story; S3: Feast; S7: Story and Snack; S8 & S9: Story, Clover Project; GB: Words for Wise, fact, and activity pages	ask lots of questions/make lots of observations about the world around them.
	Girls develop critical thinking.	recognize that the thoughts and feelings of others can vary from their own.	S2 and S3: Opening, Role-Play, Closing; S9: Opening; S10: Words and Deeds; GB: all differences among flower friends	make statements that show they recognize another's feelings or opinions.
CONNECT	Girls develop healthy relationships.	are better able to demonstrate helpful and caring behavior.	S1, S2: Role-Play; S4: Deeds; GB: All chapters	spontaneously offer to help someone in need of assistance (e.g., opening door, carrying package).
		are better able to identify and communicate their feelings to others.	S1, S3: Role-Play; GB: All conversations among the flower friends	express their feelings verbally rather than nonverbally.
	Girls promote cooperation and team-building.	begin to learn how to work well with others.	S1, S2, S3: Role-Play, Blue Bucket Award; S4, S5, S6: Firefly Award; GB: Teamwork among the flower friends	name something about themselves that helps them work well in a group (e.g., "I listen well").
	Girls can resolve conflicts.	begin to understand what conflict is.	S1: Role-Play; GB: All mentions of Yellow Lupine and White Sweetclover: Chapter 1, p. 16; Chapter 2, p. 32; Chapter 6	give examples of conflict situations in their lives.
		learn simple conflict-resolution strategies.	S1: Role-Play, Taking a Walk; GB: Chapter 3, Chapter 6	express feelings using "I statements" when they find themselves in a conflict situation.
	Girls advance diversity in a multicultural world.	recognize that it's OK to be different.	All Sessions: Opening ceremonies; GB: All flower friends, Tatiana, and Jaz	identify characteristics that make them different from other girls.
		increasingly relate to others in an inclusive manner.	S3: Role-Play; GB: Flower friends behavior among themselves and toward others	notice when others are excluded from activities.
	Girls feel connected to their communities.	are better able to identify community people/places and understand their contributions.	GB: All women and girl profiles	identify people who provide services in their communities.
TAKE ACTION	Girls are resourceful problem solvers.	learn the basics of planning a project.	S7, S8: Clover Project	with adult guidance, make a list of resources needed to complete their project.
	Girls advocate for themselves and others.	recognize that they can act on behalf of others.	S1, S2, S3: Role-Play; S7, S8, S9: Clover Project; GB: All chapters	recognize situations when they can "make something better" for someone else.
	Girls feel empowered to make a difference.	feel their actions and words are important to others.	S1, S2, S3: Role-Play; S7, S8, S9: Clover Project; GB: All chapters	give an example of something they have done to make them feel like an important part of their group.

S=Session, GB=Girls' Book

Seeing Processes and Outcomes Play Out in the Journey

Girl Scout processes play out in a variety of ways during team gatherings, but often they are so seamless you might not notice them. For example, in Session 1 (page 45), the Daisies take part in a role-playing activity about resolving conflicts. The call-outs below show how the Girl Scout processes make this activity a learning and growing experience for girls—and up the fun, too! Throughout *Between Earth and Sky,* you'll see processes and outcomes play out again and again. Before you know it, you'll be using these valuable aspects of Girl Scouting in whatever Daisies do—from taking a romp in the great outdoors to Girl Scout Cookie Activities.

FROM SAMPLE SESSION 1

Role-Play: How Do We Settle a Conflict?

Ask the girls to volunteer to pair up and do some role-playing. The aim is to get the girls making a step forward from simply saying how they feel, as they did in their opening ceremony, to being able to take into consideration the feelings of others when they team up.

> This is a good example of **Cooperative Learning** as girls team up to focus on gaining conflict-management skills.

Start by giving the girls this scenario:

> *It's been raining all morning, but now the rain has stopped. You're at a friend's house, and you're trying to decide what to do. Your friend wants to stay indoors and draw pictures. You want to go outdoors and splash in the rain puddles. Neither of you wants to change your mind, but you both want to play together.*

> Though this is part of the same activity, this goal is directly aimed at the **Discover outcome, Girls develop critical thinking skills** as they work toward recognizing and considering that other people have thoughts and feelings that are different from their own.

Then explain the larger picture of what is happening:

> *When two people want to do different things and neither one will give in, it's called a* conflict.

So a conflict is when people disagree about something. They don't have to quarrel or use angry or loud voices or ugly words, but they have different views of the same situation. In this case, the two friends disagree about what they should do together.

Then ask: *What might you do to end this conflict, so you and your friend can play together and have a good time?*

Depending on how the girls respond, here are some possible hints to get them thinking toward a solution that the two friends might both agree to:

- *One of you might be nice enough to let your friend have her way and say, "Let's do what you want to do. Next time, we can do what I want to do."*

- *You might agree to do both things! You could first go splash in some puddles and then come inside, dry off, and draw pictures together.*

- *You might agree to do something else altogether, like playing games with a younger brother and teaching him something you've learned in school.*

Ask: *How does it feel to find a way to make yourself and your friend happy?*

If you have time, ask the girls to offer their own examples of times when compromising like this is a good idea.

Then say: *When you work out things like this with a friend, it's called compromising. That's a good way to get along with people. On this journey, we're going to collect good ways to talk with one another and good ways to get along. We're going to collect them all in our blue bucket—like the blue buckets we'll see the flowers riding in when we hear the story of their road trip.*

This explanation is perfectly designed to fit the **Connect outcome, Girls can resolve conflicts**, at the Daisy level. In this exercise, girls are learning the meaning of conflict and how to identify a conflict when they see one. The activity also helps girls learn basic conflict-resolution strategies.

This activity of learning various ways to compromise is both **Cooperative Learning** and **Learning by Doing.**

In a compromise, girls recognize that what they say and do affects other people so significantly that they must reconsider their position if everyone is to be satisfied in the end. This consideration and recognition of their actions on the feelings of others is aimed at the **Discover outcome, Girls develop positive values.**

Compromising, especially among friends in scenarios such as this, is an act of caring, and therefore this activity is focused on the caring aspect of the **Connect outcome, Girls develop healthy relationships.** At the very foundation of teamwork is compromise, so the **Connect outcome, Girls promote cooperation and team-building,** is supported here as girls learn to work well with others through compromise.

From the *Daisy Flower Garden* to *Between Earth and Sky*

DON'T GIVE AWAY THE STORY!

If *Between Earth and Sky* is the first Girl Scout leadership journey your Daisy group is taking, skip these leadership links. You wouldn't want to spoil the story of *Welcome to the Daisy Flower Garden* before the girls have a chance to enjoy it from start to finish. Just go ahead and enjoy *Between Earth and Sky.*

WHERE ARE THE DAISY GIRLS?

If you and your group of Daisies enjoyed the first leadership journey with Campbell, Cora, and Chandra, you (and they) may be wondering why they're not in this journey, too.

Well, those Daisy friends couldn't take a long road trip right now, but the Daisies are welcome to add them in. What would they like the three Daisy friends to be doing in the story?

Better yet, what would the real Daisies like to do if *they* could travel with the flowers? Maybe some older girls can team up with them to add in some story scenes.

If your group of Girl Scout Daisies has already enjoyed the *Welcome to the Daisy Flower Garden*, keep those experiences growing by linking some of its "key" leadership ideas to the *Between Earth and Sky* adventures.

You might talk to the girls about how their *Daisy Flower Garden* experiences also put them on an adventure with the flower friends. For example, you might ask the girls:

- *Which flowers do you remember from our first journey?*
- *Which flowers were your favorites?*
- *What do the flower friends teach you?* (Answer: *The Girl Scout Law!*)
- *Who remembers Daisy? Which lines of the Law does she represent?* (Answer: *All!*) *Have you ever lived all of the lines?*
- *Who remembers Sandy's Song? Who can sing it for us?*

You may find that the Daisies enjoy repeating the opening ceremonies or some of the activities of *Welcome to the Daisy Flower Garden*. And if the Daisies enjoyed writing a message to the next year's Daisies, assist them in writing one about this journey, too!

Your Perspective on Leadership

The Girl Scout Leadership philosophy—Discover + Connect + Take Action—implies that leadership happens from the inside out. Your thoughts, enthusiasm, and approach will influence the Daisies, so take some time to reflect on your own perspective on leadership. Take a few minutes now—and throughout *Between Earth and Sky*—to apply the three "keys" of leadership to yourself.

| Discover | ✚ | Connect | ✚ | Take Action | ＝ | Leadership |

DISCOVER What values do you hold related to caring for the environment? Is it ever hard to act on them? Why? What does the Girl Scout Law line "use resources wisely" mean to you?

_____

_____

_____

CONNECT Who would you like to add to your community network? Why do you think it's important for Daisies to connect with an expanding network of people?

_____

_____

_____

TAKE ACTION How does your role as a volunteer with Girl Scout Daisies contribute to making the world—and specifically the environment—better?

_____

_____

_____

Identifying Journey "Helpers"

As on any Girl Scout journey, you don't have to do everything alone! You'll get a break and expand the girls' awareness of community by asking the family members, friends, and friends of friends to visit the Daisies.

So go ahead and "hand off" activities and prep steps to the Daisy Friends and Family Network. Before *Between Earth and Sky* begins, aim for a brief get-together (even online!) with parents, caregivers, relatives, and friends. Find out who likes to do what, identify assistants for various journey activities, and see who has time for behind-the-scenes preparations, gathering supplies (pads, markers, glitter, glue), or journey-themed snack duty. Keep in mind that in some families, an aunt, older sibling, cousin, grandparent, or other adult may be most able to participate.

As part of *Between Earth and Sky,* the Daisies will choose a natural treasure in their community to learn about and protect. (This will be happening in Sessions 8 and 9.) It's important to let the Daisies decide as much as possible about their projects, but you'll find it helpful to identify contacts in the community ahead of time. Then, once the Daisies are ready to move ahead, you'll have a head start on who might be able to assist them.

Pages 33–35 offer various letters and forms to get your Network started and to keep members informed and involved all along *Between Earth and Sky*:

- Welcome Letter
- Checklist for the Friends and Family Network
- Take-Home Letter for help with journey snacks
- Take-Home Letter for help with art supplies

MAKING THE NETWORK WORK

Use the Daisy Friends and Family Network forms as a handy way to inform everyone of the special needs of the Daisy journey. The forms, which can be photocopied, can also be found online at girlscouts. org. You can always reach out to the Network in less formal but "greener" ways— e-mail, phone, in-person chats. You might even make your own forms on reused or recycled paper.

Welcome! Help Make Your Daisy's Experience Bloom with Possibilities

Dear Daisy Friends and Family Network:

Your Girl Scout Daisy has joined a team of girls on a journey *Between Earth and Sky*.

As the girls explore the world's great landscapes and the positive values of the Girl Scout Law, they will also be practicing and developing communications and observation skills.

Your active participation can make the girls' experience even more valuable and memorable. Please take a moment to review the enclosed checklist to tell us which areas you might know something about (or be willing to learn), or have time to volunteer for, so that the Daisies will have the richest experience possible.

Then please identify on the enclosed Clover Project Possibilities list any natural treasure in your community that might benefit from the Daisies' learning and care. What's the Clover project? It's a way for the girls to learn to use resources wisely—using resources wisely is Clover's line of the Girl Scout Law—and protect a natural treasure!

If you have any community contacts who might like to assist, let us know that, too. Remember, a treasure can be small!

The girls and I look forward to hearing from you—and seeing you at Daisy gatherings throughout the journey.

Sincerely,

Daisy Friends and Family Checklist

Please have your Daisy return this form at her next Girl Scout gathering.

☐ **YES! I WANT TO HELP THE DAISIES GROW.** I or someone I know can assist with:

_____ Transportation

_____ Snacks (with an "earthy" theme!)

_____ Science activities

_____ Meeting supplies (markers, paper, crayons, pads, markers, glitter, glue—nothing fancy; reuse and recycle as much as possible)

_____ Ideas for learning about protecting a local natural treasure

_____ The *Between Earth and Sky* final celebration

_____ Nature walks and other trips

_____ Some of the Daisy gatherings

My name: _____   My Daisy's name: _____

My phone: _____   My e-mail: _____

☐ **YES! I have CONTACTS IN THE COMMUNITY WHO COULD HELP.** They are:

Name: _____   Name: _____

Contact info: _____   Contact info: _____

Name: _____   Name: _____

Contact info: _____   Contact info: _____

☐ **YES! I KNOW OF GOOD CLOVER PROJECT POSSIBILITIES IN OUR COMMUNITY.**
They are:

1. _____   4. _____

2. _____   5. _____

3. _____   6. _____

Assist Your Daisy in Her Journey!

Dear Girl Scout Daisy Family:

Your Girl Scout Daisy is hitting the road for a Girl Scout leadership journey.

To make the journey as enjoyable as possible, the Daisy Family and Friends Network is being called on to supply creative snacks for each Daisy gathering.

Earthy snacks like fruits and vegetables will make the best journey snacks. And several gatherings call for specific treats that match the day's theme.

Please let us know the dates of those Daisy gatherings you can help with.

Thank you!

Assist Your Daisy in Her Journey!

Dear Girl Scout Daisy Family:

Your Girl Scout Daisy is on the Girl Scout leadership journey *Between Earth and Sky*.

To get started, your Daisy will be helping to build a team flower friends' road trip poster using cut paper images. This creative picture will be based on the girls' ideas and imaginations.

Beside making images from cut paper, the girls can also write, draw, and paint on the poster. Your assistance with creative materials will make the girls' poster truly exciting.

The Daisies will appreciate any colored scrap paper, magazines, photos, crayons, colored pens and pencils, bits of fabric or foil, or any creative materials you can contribute. Feel feel to let your Daisy bring them to her next Girl Scout gathering.

Thank you!

LET THE FLOWERS INSPIRE THE DAISIES

The Daisies might enjoy knowing that the artist who created the flower friends in their book likes to make pictures out of cut paper. And they might like to make pictures from cut paper, too.

Sample Session 2 suggests that you get the girls started on a team poster that captures all their adventures on this journey. But they must follow this one rule: All the pictures they place on the poster must be pieced together from cut paper!

With your Daisy Network, get a box (or bucket!) going of colorful scrap paper that the girls can use to create their pictures. And give them the page of flower friends at right (also available online at girlscouts.org) as inspiration! By the journey's final celebration, the girls are sure to have a masterpiece to show their families and other guests.

The Artist Behind the Journey's Pictures

The artist behind the colorful pictures in *Between Earth and Sky* is Susan Swan, a master of creating images from cut paper.

Swan was born in Coral Gables, Florida, and grew up in the Lake Worth/Palm Beach area. Each summer, her family spent two weeks in the Florida Keys. "My brother and I could collect shells from the beautiful white sandy beaches and watch gorgeously colored tropical fish swim by in brilliant blue and green water," she says. "Beautiful water and palm-tree-studded beaches still make me happy today."

Swan studied art in college and graduate school but didn't get started with cut paper until working for a Westport, Connecticut, design studio that produced many textbooks. Throughout her career, Swan has worked in all sorts of art—watercolor, scratch board, pen and ink. "I've always liked to try new things, to experiment," she says.

Cut paper has become her trademark. As her designs became more complicated, she grew tired of rushing to deadline. "The studio would become a huge mess of little bits of paper left over from cutting out the shapes. Now I work digitally and totally love it." She still creates some things by hand, and paints many paper patterns which she then scans into her computer to use in her images.

"I work in a little studio behind our house in a tiny town called Ovilla, in Texas," she says. "When I have the time I like to be in the garden," she adds. "We have put in lots of flower and even vegetable beds around our house." She also likes to do collage and crafty things, and read.

Her favorite travel destination right now? Asheville, North Carolina. "It is filled with artists and crafters and very beautiful scenery," she says.

And her favorite food? "TEX-Mex, of course! Cheese, spinach, mushrooms, onions, peppers in any combination—*quesadillas*, salsa made from the garden, chili, stuffed zucchini, *chiles rellenos*, tortilla soup."

The Flower Friends and Their Girl Scout Law Values

Hello, I'm **Sunny, the sunflower.** I'm from Great Britain and I'm friendly and helpful. I join the road trip in Pittsburgh.

Hi, I'm **Daisy.** I represent all parts of the Girl Scout Law. The Daisy Flower Garden is named for me—and for all Girl Scout Daisies, including Girl Scouts founder Juliette "Daisy" Gordon Low.

Hi, I'm **Lupe, the lupine.** I'm blue and honest and fair. I love to summer in Maine. I'm in the driver's seat on this road trip.

Hi, I'm **Zinni, the zinnia.** I'm spring green and considerate and caring. I'm from Mexico and I'm Lupe's first passenger on this trip.

Hi, I'm **Mari, the marigold.** I'm orange and "responsible for what I say and do." I stay home in the Daisy Flower Garden.

Hi, I'm **Tula, the tulip.** I'm red and courageous and strong. I'm from Holland. I join the road trip in Washington State.

Hi, I'm **Gerri, the geranium.** I'm magenta and I respect authority. I stay home in the Daisy Flower Garden.

Hi, I'm **Gloria, the morning glory.** I'm purple and I "respect myself and others." My flower friends visit me in Maine.

Hello, I'm **Clover.** I'm green with white flowers. I use resources wisely. I join the road trip, too—to get to Alaska.

Hi, I'm **Vi, the violet.** I'm "a sister to every Girl Scout." I'm from Australia. I stay home in the Daisy garden, too.

Hi, I'm **Rosie, the rose.** I like to "make the world a better place." I join the road trip in California.

Nature "is written in the language of mathematics . . . its characters are triangles, circles, and other geometrical figures . . . "

— Galileo, Italian physicist, mathematician, astronomer, and philosopher, 1564-1642

The Journey's 10 Sample Sessions

The Sample Sessions in this guide show how to organize *Between Earth and Sky* into 10 gatherings with girls. But if you have the time, don't rush. This journey is intended to develop the girls' love for the natural world and all its wonders—while they live the Girl Scout Law.

So feel free to add in additional sessions, particularly if you are devoting extended time to the flower friends' story or to enjoying the great outdoors.

Activities in the Sample Sessions elaborate on environmental and leadership themes touched on in the girls' book. To assist you, session plans often point to specific passages that will enrich your gatherings with the girls.

Science is also built right into every sample session, through activities that have the girls observing, communicating, and classifying. So as the Daisies practice leadership skills and values, they also move forward as budding scientists! Throughout the journey, you will guide the girls to:

- use all their senses to gather information
- use words and drawings to describe, name, record, and share
- create order in groups of objects by finding their similarities and differences

Observing, communicating, and classifying are basic process skills of science. This journey shows how essential they are to so many things in daily life—and how much fun they can be!

What You'll Find in Each Session

AT A GLANCE: The session's goal, activities, and a list of simple materials you'll need.

What to Say: Examples of what to say and ask the Daisies along the journey as you link activities, reflections, and learning experiences. Must you read from the "script"? Absolutely not! The girls (and you!) will have far more fun if you take the main ideas from the examples provided and then just be yourself.

Activity Instructions: Tips for guiding the girls through activities and experiences along *Between Earth and Sky*, and plenty of "tools" (activity sheets, family letters, etc.) to support the experiences on the journey.

Coaching to Create a Quality Experience: The quality of the Girl Scout Leadership Experience depends greatly on three processes—Girl Led, Cooperative Learning, and Learning by Doing. By following the prompts in this guide for activities, reflections, girl choice-making, and discussions, you'll be using the processes with ease.

Tying Activities to Impact: This guide notes the purpose of the journey's activities and discussions, so you'll always understand the intended benefit to girls. And you'll even be able to see the benefits—by observing the "signs" that the girls are achieving the Girl Scout National Leadership Outcomes.

Thinking and Speaking: The role-play activities and reflections featured in the sample sessions are designed to encourage and build the Daisies' communication skills. They tie directly to the journey's leadership outcomes and offer a direct way to see the Girl Scout processes of Learning by Doing and Cooperative Learning in action.

SUGGESTIONS, NOT MUST-DO'S

If you're wondering whether you "must" do each activity or ceremony, you can usually presume the answer is no! This guide is full of suggestions for ways to give girls the Girl Scout experience of leadership. Do what's best for your Daisy group.

STUCK INDOORS? NOT TO WORRY!

It's always best if the girls can get out to enjoy the great outdoors firsthand. Nature, after all, is the backbone of this journey.

But if that's just not possible, given the climate, time of day, or other circumstances in your region, just bring some nature indoors! Take your cue from the suggestions for adapting "Taking a Walk, Outdoors or In" in Sample Session 1 and apply them to other activities along the journey as needed.

Customizing the Journey

Think of these sample sessions as the main route through *Between Earth and Sky*—they will get you and the girls from each step to the next, accomplishing goals along the way. As on any journey, if you and your passengers have the time, venture off the main route now and then to see in real life all that is *Between Earth and Sky*!

FIELD TRIPS AND THE GREAT OUTDOORS

With assistance from the Daisy Friends and Family Network, you and the girls might visit local parks, preserves, and gardens to explore an array of natural wonders. People who work at these locations will have wonderful information to share with the girls. You might also visit sites where the Daisies can identify a local "treasure" they want to protect—an activity toward earning the Clover Award. A treasure can be a plant, a bird, or a place. It can be as simple as a tree trying to grow near the girls' Daisy meeting space or something bigger, like an area in a state park. The goal is to give the girls a chance to explore important environmental issues, and spark conversations about how they can help protect nature.

Experiencing nature firsthand gives the Daisies opportunities to deepen their love and respect for Planet Earth. So, whenever possible, invite the girls into the great outdoors. If you have access to outdoor space in the community or through your council, enjoy it as much as possible.

MAKING THINGS

Many Daisies love to create, so depending on their interests, add a little time to a session (or add a whole session) to make a craft, try a simple recipe, or experiment with other projects that girls can give as gifts or enjoy themselves. And don't feel you need to do it all yourself. Ask "crafty" parents or other relatives to assist with projects related to the theme of the day's meeting. For example, perhaps some Girl Scout Juniors can assist the Daisies with their origami project in Session 4. As the Daisies learn from the older girls, the older girls will be building leadership skills, too.

FLOWER FRIENDSHIPS

As your Girl Scout Daisy group enjoyed the flower friends in *Welcome to the Daisy Flower Garden*, perhaps each girl chose a specific flower to "befriend" along the way. If so, invite the girls to continue that friendship in *Between Earth and Sky*. Or perhaps the girls would like to choose a new flower to bring along for the ride!

SAMPLE SESSION 1
Getting Ready for the Road

This first Session introduces the Daisies to the joys of travel and asks them to share their travel experiences.

The discussion that you guide the girls through encourages them to consider how their likes and dislikes might vary, and how natural that diversity is.

Together, these activities open the way to "A Road Trip to Remember," the story at the heart of this leadership journey.

AT A GLANCE

Goal: The girls begin to express their feelings and start to understand and experience the joys of travel, especially outdoors in nature.

- Opening Ceremony: "Have a Good Trip!" and How I'm Feeling

- Story Time: Travel Near, Travel Far

- Role-Play: How Do We Settle a Conflict?

- Taking a Walk, Indoors or Out

- Which One Is Mine?

- Closing Ceremony: How We're Feeling and a Friendship Squeeze

- Looking Ahead to Session 2

MATERIALS

- **Opening Ceremony:** recycled cardboard or construction paper (for making luggage tags/bookmarks); background patches for the Daisies' leadership awards (optional)

- **Story Time:** the girls' book

- **Girl Scout Promise:** whiteboard or chalkboard or large sheet of paper (recycled is best!)

- **Taking a Walk:** access to an outdoor spot with fallen leaves, twigs, seeds, or nuts (or a variety of these items spread around the meeting place of the Daisies, enough for all the girls)

- **Which One Is Mine?:** paper and crayons or markers, enough for all the girls

- **Closing Ceremony:** chalkboard, whiteboard, or paper and markers; or a blue bucket; or any recycled container, and various supplies for the girls to decorate it to be the team's blue bucket

PREPARE AHEAD

Chat with any assistants about what they'll do before and during the session.

If the group won't be "Taking a Walk" outdoors, scatter natural materials (leaves, twigs, acorns) around the meeting room, where the girls can easily find them. Be sure to have enough of each item for all the girls to have one—they will make a team decision about which item they will "collect."

AS GIRLS ARRIVE

Invite them to look through their book, especially the first few pages of the flower friends' story. If you're using a recycled container for the team's blue bucket, invite the girls to decorate it with any art supplies on hand.

Opening Ceremony: Have a Good Trip!

Once all the girls arrive, gather them into a circle, and if they are new to Girl Scouting, explain that they are now in a Daisy Circle, something they will form to mark special times, such as:

- starting their Girl Scout Daisy gatherings
- welcoming new girls and special visitors
- sharing thoughts and ideas
- making group decisions
- listening to the flower friends' story, "A Road Trip to Remember"
- any other times they want to talk as a group

IF YOUR DAISY GROUP IS NEW TO GIRL SCOUTING . . .

Ask the girls to celebrate their Daisy Circle by saying hello and introducing themselves one by one—by saying their name and how they feel today. Start by example, saying something like, "Hi, my name is Tamar, and I am so excited today. I'm really looking forward to starting this Girl Scout journey with all of you!" The girls may need prompting, so be ready with simple questions like, "Do you feel happy about being in this Daisy gathering today? Is anyone excited to be here? Did anyone wear something special to celebrate this first Daisy gathering? Is anyone nervous—just a little?"

MEMENTOS FROM NATURE

The natural items that the girls collect in this first session will be the first of many mementos of the journey.

Encourage the Daisies to save all the treasures they find and make along the journey so they can share them with friends and guests at their closing celebration—and treasure them long after the journey ends. There's even a special place on the final page of their book where they can paste their favorites.

IF THE GIRLS ALREADY KNOW ONE ANOTHER . . .

Go around the circle and have each girl say how she's been feeling since the Daisies last got together.

After this opening circle, let the girls know how great it is that they are talking about how they feel. Explain that they will share even more about how they feel and how they think others feel during more of their Daisy time together.

Take time now to put a new twist on the tradition the Daisies started if they enjoyed the leadership journey *Welcome to the Daisy Flower Garden*: learning key phrases in a variety of languages. Let the girls know that today they will try out the phrase "Have a great trip," because they are all starting a journey together.

You might say: *We're about to start a journey called* Between Earth and Sky. *In this journey, we're going to hear a story about some pretty flower friends taking a trip across the country. We're going to see everything they see. The story is called "A Road Trip to Remember."*

Then ask:

- *Have you ever taken a trip or watched someone leave on a trip?*
- *What did people say to you when you were leaving? Or what did you say to the people who were about to travel?*

If the girls don't have an answer, say: *Did anyone say, "Have a good trip!" That's a nice and polite thing to say when people travel. In fact, people all around the world say that to each other. As we follow the flower friends on their road trip, we're going to learn how to say "Have a good trip!" in many ways—just as people do all around the world. And we're going to start with English!*

Now, let's all say it to one another together! Ready? "HAVE A GOOD TRIP!"

Then pass out the Daisies' road trip patches (the background for their leadership awards) and also invite the girls to begin making their own journey-long luggage tag or bookmark that they will decorate with the phrase "Have a good trip" in all the languages they learn. Pass out the cardboard or paper and crayons and markers and let the girls get to it!

LIVING THE LAW!

Let the girls know that saying "Have a good trip!" is a way of being friendly—and being friendly is one way to live the Girl Scout Law.

You might ask if any of the Daisies know which of the flower friends represents being friendly.

Answer: *Sunny, the sunflower!*

Story Time: Travel Near, Travel Far

Next, introduce the new flower friends story by reading the short introduction on page 5 of the girls' book, pausing at the end of each paragraph to ask a question or two to spark the girls' thinking. Here are some suggestions (you don't have to use them all—and feel free to ask your own questions, too!):

- *How many of you have traveled to faraway places? Where did you go? What did you see?*

- *What do you remember packing for your trip?*

- *How many of you like to take short trips in your neighborhood? Raise your hands if you do!*

- *Where do you like to go the most?*

- *How about when it's raining? Do you like to travel in the rain? What do you wear to stay dry?*

- *How do you think it's possible to travel very far without any suitcase at all? What does that mean?*

Depending on the Daisies' answers to that last question, say something like:

- *On this journey, we'll be traveling through a story. And this story is make-believe. So we won't need any suitcases at all. We just need to listen closely and enjoy everything that happens to the flowers on their trip.*

- *We have plenty of pictures in our book to help us "see" everything the flowers friends do!*

- *And after we hear each part of the story, we'll also get to enjoy all that's* Between Earth and Sky—*by going outdoors just like the flower friends!*

Role-Play: How Do We Settle a Conflict?

Ask the girls to volunteer to pair up and do some role-playing. The aim is to get them to move beyond simply saying how they feel, as they did in the opening ceremony, to consider the feelings of others when they team up.

Start by giving the girls this scenario:

> *It's been raining all morning, but now the rain has stopped. You're at a friend's house, and you're trying to decide what to do. Your friend wants to stay indoors and draw pictures. You want to go outdoors and splash in the rain puddles. Neither of you wants to change your mind, but you both want to play together.*

DAISY DISCUSSIONS & REFLECTIONS

Engaging girls in discussions about the importance of good speaking skills in their lives helps them reflect on what they experience in their Daisy gathering and apply it to their own lives. So keep that Daisy chatter going! It's truly a purposeful experience.

TOWARD THE AWARD AND LEADERSHIP FOR GIRLS!

This role-play activity, and others throughout the journey, are meant to give girls practice and confidence in communication skills, specifically ways to resolve conflicts through negotiation, compromise, and being considerate of one another—all of which tie to the national Girl Scout leadership **Discover outcome, Girls can resolve conflicts.**

The Daisies build on these skills during the first three sessions of the journey to earn the Blue Bucket Award. But they continue to practice them throughout the journey.

Then explain the larger picture of what's happening:

> *When two people want to do different things and neither one will give in, it's called a* conflict.

> *So a conflict is when people disagree about something. They don't have to quarrel or use angry or loud voices or ugly words, but they have different views of the same situation. In this case, the two friends disagree about what they should do together.*

Then ask: *What might you do to try to end to this conflict so you and your friend can play together and have a good time?*

Depending on how the girls respond, here are some possible hints to get them thinking toward a solution that the two friends might both agree to:

- *One of you might be nice enough to let your friend have her way and say, "Let's do what you want to do. Next time, we can do what I want to do."*

- *You might agree to do both things! You could first go splash in some puddles and then come inside, dry off, and draw pictures together.*

- *You might agree to do something else altogether, like playing games with a younger brother and teaching him something you've learned in school.*

Ask: *How does it feel to find a way to make yourself and your friend happy?*

If you have time, ask the girls to offer their own examples of times when compromising like this is a good idea.

Then say: *When you work out things like this with a friend, it's called compromising. That's a good way to get along with people. On this journey, we're going to collect good ways to talk with one another and good ways to get along. We're going to collect them all in our blue bucket—like the blue buckets we'll see the flowers riding in when we hear the story of their road trip.*

Capture the girls' ideas on the lines above your blue bucket on page 49.

Taking a Walk, Outdoors or In

If possible, get the girls outside for a short romp in nature. While out, have the girls each collect one natural item. The only catch is they must all collect the same type of item, such as a fallen leaf or pinecone or acorn. So first, the girls must make a group decision about what they will collect. Let them know that when they're back inside, they'll draw the item they've collected.

To get a team decision going, you might ask: *Who has an idea about what we should collect?*

If the girls have many ideas, guide them to reach a group decision. You might ask: *Who is willing to change her mind about what we should collect? Who can offer a good reason for some of us to change our minds?*

Help guide the girls to make a team decision. Check for any bruised feelings if the team decision doesn't go the way some girls wanted.

Before this first outdoor excursion with the Daisies, take some time to explain Leave No Trace practices, as detailed on page 20 of this guide.

Which One Is Mine?

Once the girls are back from their romp outside, have them sketch their item using crayons and paper. This is a great activity to introduce the idea of careful observation as well as using all of one's senses, so ask the girls to pay close attention to any unique features their item has. For example, if the girls collected leaves, do any of the leaves have a bite out of them? If they chose acorns, are any of them more long than round? If they collected pinecones, do any have seeds falling out of them or animal fur stuck to them?

Encourage the girls to touch their objects, so they learn how they feel as well as how they look. Their crayon-and-paper renderings don't have to be exact or detailed. The idea is for the girls to capture their feeling for the object.

When their sketches are done, have the girls turn them over and then come sit in a circle and put their natural items in the center. Get them talking about what they learned about their item. Ask: *Were there any surprises? Was there something new you hadn't noticed before?*

Then ask the girls to scatter their sketches in the center of where they are sitting, too. Say:

- *Now, as a group, can you match the objects to the sketches?*

- *How many can you match? (Don't count your own, and don't give away which one is yours!)*

- *What makes it easy or hard to match the real things to the drawings?*

HOW DID IT FEEL TO BE OUTDOORS?

When the Daisies return from their time outdoors, be sure to ask them:

How did it feel to out and about just like the flower friends—in the fresh air Between Earth and Sky?

ART FOR ALL!

Keep in mind that each girl is likely to have her own unique way of drawing the natural item the group "collected."

So no comparisons and no judging! That makes for no worries!

Remind the girls that being friendly and considerate when viewing each others' drawings is living the Girl Scout Law.

You might ask: *Do you remember which flower friend is friendly, and which is considerate?* (Answer: *Sunny and Zinni!*)

NEW DAISIES— OR NOT?

If the Daisies are new to Girl Scouting, see page 23 in this guide to explain a Friendship Circle and squeeze. If some Daisies already know how to create a Friendship Circle and squeeze, invite them to teach any newcomers.

DAISIES AND CEREMONIES

Keep in mind that it may prove challenging for the Daisies to suggest their own ceremonies. That's OK! At their age, repeating a closing ceremony from meeting to meeting will be a welcome tradition.

Closing Ceremony: How We're Feeling and a Friendship Squeeze

Ask the girls to join together again in a Daisy Circle. Then invite them to go around the circle and say how they're feeling now after this first Daisy journey session. Are they happy? Excited? Tired? Capture all the words the Daisies say and add them to your blue bucket on the next page. If you have a large version of the bucket on a chalkboard or on poster board or newsprint, add them there as well, so the girls can see them. Or, better yet, write them on slips of paper and keep them in an actual bucket—or the container the girls decorated to be their blue bucket.

Then invite the Daisies to close their time together with a Friendship Circle and a friendship squeeze. Let them know that adults call this kind of thing a closing ceremony. Explain that the word "ceremony" means celebrating something in a special way—they're celebrating the time they spent together today as Girl Scouts. Let the girls know that they can think up their own ceremonies all along the journey.

Thank the girls for a great first Girl Scout Daisy gathering on this *Between Earth and Sky* journey. Encourage them to enjoy their book before their next Daisy gathering, and to share it with their families, too. Finally, let them know that you look forward to their next Girl Scout time together.

Looking Ahead to Session 2

The next session's "Science Time" activity focuses on the textures and smells of fresh soil (also see page 8 in the girls' book). You and the Daisy Friends and Family Network can likely gather soil samples. But if you invite a gardener or farmer to visit with the girls, you'll have a soil expert to assist in creating a fun and informative "soil show."

Session 2 is also a good time to get the girls started on a team poster made from colorful cut paper. See page 36 in this guide on how to use the pictures in their book, and the artist who made them, to inspire the girls. You and they can decide when to work on the poster—at the start of each gathering, in the middle, or at the close.

Also, you may want a guest reader for the next gathering's story segment!

Blue Bucket of Words
COLLECTING GOOD WAYS TO TALK, AND FEELINGS

SAMPLE SESSION 2
Our Road Trip Begins

AT A GLANCE

Goal: Girls continue to explore what makes them unique as they start to consider the feelings of their sister Daisies and expand their knowledge of shapes in nature.

- Opening Ceremony: Have a Great Trip (French and Turkish) and How Are You Feeling?

- Story Time

- Role-Play: How I Help My Friends

- Science Time: The Sweet Smell of Soil

- A Walk in Nature to Find Colors

- Closing Ceremony: I Think You're Feeling . . .

- Looking Ahead to Session 3

MATERIALS

- **As Girls Arrive:** paper, scissors, and drawing materials

- **Opening Ceremony:** crayons, markers and decorative bits

- **Story Time:** the girls' book and this guide

- **A Walk in Nature:** newsprint and easel or individual sheets of paper for the girls and crayons or markers

PREPARE AHEAD

Look over the first chapter of the girls' book to familiarize yourself with the start of the story and the picture of Lupe's petal-power car.

Chat with any assistants about what they'll do before and during the session.

AS GIRLS ARRIVE

Invite them to flip through their book. Which pictures do they like? Do they want to get started on a team journey poster (see pages 36 and 48).

Opening Ceremony: Have a Great Trip (French and Turkish) and How Are You Feeling?

Have the girls gather in a Daisy Circle. Let them know that today they will say "Have a great trip" to one another in French, a language known by Mari, the marigold, but also used by many English-speaking people. In French, "Have a good trip" is *Bon voyage! Bon voyage* is also used in Turkish, so Tula the tulip, whose family is originally from Turkey, might know the phrase, too. Mari, by the way, is not a passenger on the road trip. Let the girls know that she stays home in the Daisy Flower Garden, so she would certainly send off her friends with a wave and *Bon voyage!*

Now ask the girls to go around the circle so that each girl can say *Bon voyage* to the girl to her right. Once the girls have completed the circle, have them all say it together. Then invite them to add *Bon voyage!* to their luggage tag/bookmark with crayons, markers, and any decorative bits on hand.

Next, let the Daisies know they have a special job today. Say something like:

- *Remember how we talked about how we were feeling when we last got together? Well, today we will pay attention to how other people feel.*

- *You are all going to pay careful attention to the girl who's now on your right. Can everyone turn to the right? Good!*

- *Now throughout our time together today, you will try to tell how that girl on your right is feeling. Is she happy? Sad? Tired? Excited? Bored?*

- *At the end of our time together, you'll say how you thought she was feeling today. And then she'll let us know if you were right!*

WORDS FOR THE WISE

SPRUCE means to make something neat. Spruce is also a kind of tree. It's an evergreen. It stays green all year long.

BUILDING DAISIES' WORD POWER

You'll notice that Chapter 1 of the road trip story features the word *spruce*.

You might ask if this is a new word for the girls. Do they know other words that mean "make neat"?

Ask them to finish this sentence: *Yesterday, my dad told me to _____ my room.*

How many words can they come up with to fill in the blank?

Story Time

Today's the day to dip into Chapter 1 of "A Road Trip to Remember." This chapter starts off with Lupe getting her car ready for a trip and Zinni wanting to help her. Read, or have any assigned helpers read, pages 7 and 8, and then page 12 up to and including the paragraph where Lupe says, "I'm sprucing up my car. I'm getting ready for a road trip."

Then show the girls the picture of Lupe's car and all its special features. Here are some questions to guide a discussion with the Daisies:

- *What do you think of Lupe's car? Does it look fun to ride in?*

- *What parts of the car do you recognize from nature?*

- *What parts of the car have you never seen before?*

- *Did you notice how the car is the same color as Lupe?*

- *If you could build a car, what would it be like? What color would it be?*

Role Play: How I Help My Friends

Ask the girls to pair up and do some role-playing. As the girls continue to polish their communication skills, they also focus on demonstrating helpful and caring behavior, which directly relates to the national Girl Scout leadership Connect outcome, Girls develop healthy relationships, something the girls will build on throughout the journey.

Start by reminding the girls of the part of the story in which Zinni is said to like to help her friend, Lupe. Then ask for two girls to volunteer to role-play. Given them this scenario: *You and your mom stop at your best friend's house to pick her up and walk to school together. Your friend is running late. She's rushing to get ready and she seems upset. What do you do?*

Depending on how the girls respond, here are some possible hints to get them thinking about how best to be helpful and caring:

- *Would you yell at your friend and say things like "Hurry up!" "We can't wait for you!" "Why aren't you ready?"*

- *Or would you tell her not to rush and that's it's OK to be a little late?*

- *Would you offer to make sure she has everything she needs? Her lunch? Her backpack? Her gloves and hat if it's cold out?*

- *What else might you do to be helpful and caring?*

Time permitting, see if the girls can suggest another "scene" that the whole group can expand into another role-play activity.

OPTION: CREATE YOUR OWN CAR

The girls might enjoy dreaming up some cars of their own and making drawings of them.

Or maybe the Daisy Network can get a treasure chest of odds and ends together that the Daisies can use to build some miniature cars. How about plastic bottle caps for wheels?

Then wrap up by getting the girls to decide on one important way to be helpful and caring. Add this to the team's blue bucket of good talking and getting along skills.

Science Time: The Sweet Smell of Soil

In the first chapter of "A Road Trip to Remember," the sweet smell of soil can be smelled inside Lupe's car. Now is a great time to let the Daisies smell that sweet smell, too. This is a chance for them to learn how fresh good soil can smell—and that they shouldn't think of soil that nurtures plants as just "dirt."

Now you (or any gardener guests) can show the girls a variety of soil samples that they can smell and touch. Aim for a range of soils that vary from sandy and dry to thick clay. Be sure to show the type of soil that is most common in your region. Explains what it's like and what it's called—and what grows well in it. No matter what type of soil your region has, aim to show the girls what rich, moist soil is like. Perhaps you can even show them some fresh compost.

A Walk in Nature to Find Colors

Before heading out with the Daisies for a walk focused on finding all the wonderful colors of nature (yes, more opportunities to observe and communicate!), ask the girls to take turns naming favorite colors.

You might even start by having them point out their favorite colorful page in their *Between Earth and Sky* book. Remind them that each flower friend is a different color, and they can see them all on the inside cover of their book.

Then have the girls draw a square of their favorite color and, if they can, also write the name of the color beside their square. Use one large sheet of paper or smaller sheets so that each girl has her own "list" of colors that represents the full Daisy group's favorites. Aim for a well-rounded list. If all the girls like blues, for example, add in your own favorite to widen the list.

If the list still isn't diverse, ask the girls to name some "fancy" colors that they might know just from using a wide assortment of crayons. You might ask:

- *Has anyone every heard of violet or magenta? How about sienna?*

Then show the girls examples of these colors. For violet and magenta, use flower friends Vi, the violet (she's violet in color) and Gerri, the geranium, who is magenta (see page 13 in this guide).

Explain to the girls that they'll now take a walk outdoors and try to find objects that match all the colors they've just named.

COLORS AND FEELINGS

The "Road Trip" story is filled with colors. You might talk with the girls about how colors are often tied to feelings. But they don't have to be!

For example, you might explain that people often think of yellow as a sunny, happy color. And they sometimes use the word *blue* to mean sad.

But Lupe, one of the flower friends in their story, is blue. And she certainly isn't sad!

Blue can also be the color of a pretty summer sky, and the color of the ocean. It's also the color of blueberries.

This is a good way for the Daisies to learn that words, and colors, can mean more than one thing!

The girls might also enjoy knowing that there are many kinds of blue! Lupe's car is powder blue, but there is also:

- royal blue
- indigo
- steel blue
- cornflower blue
- French blue
- midnight blue
- aquamarine
- turquoise

How many of these blues are in their crayon box? Where else might these blues be found?

CITIES HAVE NATURE, TOO

Even the most congested urban areas are home to parks and gardens. Check with your area's parks and planning offices to locate one near you.

The American Community Gardening Association, in Columbus, Ohio, has a database of community gardens—visit www.communitygarden.org or e-mail info@communitygarden.org.

SCIENCE SKILLS!

The girls aren't talking science here, but they're still honing the skills of science: observing and communicating are basic process skills of science.

As the girls walk, have them share what they find. At the end of the walk, get a discussion going with questions like these:

- *How many colors did you find from our list?*

- *Were there any you couldn't find?*

- *Did any colors you found outdoors surprise you at all?*

- *Did any disappoint you? In any way?*

- *Did you find any colors that you didn't know the names of?*

- *How did being outdoors in nature make you feel?*

- *How did seeing the different colors make you feel? Did you feel any different when looking at different colors?*

- *Where else might we look for colors outdoors?*

- *Do you think we could find places with even more colors? Where?*

And be sure to ask the Daisies if they have any questions!

Closing Ceremony: I Think You're Feeling . . .

Ask the girls to come together again in a Daisy Circle, in the same order they were at this gathering's opening ceremony. Then go around the circle and ask each girl to say how she thought the girl on her right was feeling today.

She might say something like, "I think Mara was happy because she was smiling all the time and laughing, too." Then Mara can say whether that was really how she was feeling, or not.

With the Daisies' help, get a list going of all the "feeling words" the girls "report." Write them on the lines above the blue bucket on the next page. If all the girls report that their sister Daisy was happy, guide the girls to learn some new words that mean happy. You might say:

- *How about cheerful? Or relaxed? Or carefree? Or easygoing?*

- *Let's see how many words we can learn and get comfortable using to express how we feel on this journey. We can add to our blue bucket every time we get together.*

And be sure to let the girls know something along these lines:

> *Keep in mind: If any of us is feeling sad or mad or unhappy, let's be sure to ask how we can help.*

> *And remember: Asking and observing how people feel is a sign that we care. Do you remember which flower friend is considerate and caring? (Answer: Zinni, the zinnia!)*

Complete the closing ceremony with a friendship squeeze. Then thank the girls for another great Daisy Girl Scout gathering. Encourage them to share their Daisy adventures with their families, and let them know you look forward to the group's next time together.

Looking Ahead to Session 3

The Science Time activity in the next session focuses on the girls getting a chance to see how plants drink water (see page 58). You and your Daisy Friends and Family Network may be able to bring in a plant or two that can stand being slightly wilted and then will perk up quickly (if you have a tomato plant in a pot, that's a good candidate). But locating a gardener or farmer to invite to the Daisy gathering will free up your time and let you enjoy a fun and informative plant drinking session, too! A gardener may also have other ideas about how to expand the girls' knowledge of how plants take in water and nutrients. After all, when the girls understand how plants drink, they learn one more thing about caring for Planet Earth!

Blue Bucket of Words
COLLECTING FEELINGS!

SAMPLE SESSION 3
You, Me, How Different We Can Be

AT A GLANCE

Goal: The girls continue to explore their feelings and how they can differ from one girl to another. They also explore the range of colors in nature.

- **Opening Ceremony: Have a Good Trip (Spanish) and Speaking Up About How We Feel**

- **Story Time**

- **Science Time: How Plants Drink**

- **Feast of Plant Parts**

- **Role-Play: I'm Feeling This and You're Feeling That**

- **Closing Ceremony: Earning the Blue Bucket Award . . .**

- **Looking Ahead to Session 4**

MATERIALS

- **As Girl Arrive:** paper and crayons for drawing

- **Opening Ceremony:** crayons or markers (for adding new decoration to luggage tags/bookmarks)

- **Science Time:** a plant, slightly droopy, that can be easily revived; water in a watering can or other container

- **A Walk in Nature:** paper, one large sheet or a small sheet for each girl; crayons in a variety of colors

PREPARE AHEAD

Chat with any assistants about what they'll do before and during the session.

AS GIRLS ARRIVE

Invite them to pick a feeling word they learned in their Daisy time together and to draw a picture of what someone feeling that way looks like. Or have them imagine what a flower friend who is feeling that way would look like!

Opening Ceremony: Have a Good Trip (Spanish) and Speaking Up About How We Feel

Have the girls gather in a Daisy Circle. Let them know that today they will say "Have a great trip" to one another in Spanish, a language known by Zinni, the zinnia, one of the main characters in their journey's story, and also by Mari, the marigold, one of flower friends who is not on the trip.

In Spanish, have a good trip is *¡Buen viaje!* Going around the circle, ask each girl to say *¡Buen viaje!* to the girl to her left. Once the girls have completed the circle, have them all say *¡Buen viaje!* again, together. Then invite them to add this phrase, or a new image, to their luggage tag/bookmark.

Then let them know they have a special job today. Say something like:

- *During our Daisy time together today, you are all going to pay attention to how you are feeling and how your sister Daisies are feeling.*

- *For example, maybe you, Tanja, are feeling excited about watering the plants that we have with us today. But you, Amy, don't want to water at all. You want to sit and enjoy the pictures in your journey book.*

- *Pay attention to what you and your sister Daisies say and do today. See if you can find someone who is feeling like you and someone who might be feeling something different. At the end of our gathering, we'll all tell one another what we noticed.*

MAKE IT GIRL LED!

If your group of Daisies includes girls from a variety of countries or cultural backgrounds, let them take the lead in deciding on a language to feature in the girls' opening ceremonies.

Story Time

Today's the day to finish Chapter 1 of "A Road Trip to Remember," starting from page 12, just ahead of where the last gathering's Story Time ended:

> *Lupe slid out from under her car and stood up.*

Lupe goes on to explain that she's traveling to Maine, and she invites Zinni and Clover to go with her.

After the reading, get a discussion going with questions like these:

You'll notice that Chapter 1 of the story features the word *considerate*. This is an important word in Girl Scouting—being considerate is part of the Girl Scout Law.

Talk with the Daisies about what being considerate means. You might start with the "Words for the Wise" definition in their book:

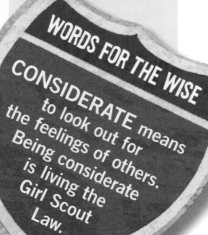

WORDS FOR THE WISE

CONSIDERATE means to look out for the feelings of others. Being considerate is living the Girl Scout Law.

Then say to the girls: *Let's think about how to be considerate to one another. Let's all agree on a way to do that in our Daisy time together and add it to our blue bucket of feelings and actions.*

You might also ask: *What other words do you know that mean considerate? Kind? Nice? What else?*

Do you remember which flower friend is considerate? (Answer: *Zinni, the zinnia!*)

- *Lupe invites Zinni and then Clover to travel with her. When have you invited friends to go somewhere with you?*

- *Have you ever not made room for other people when you're riding in a car or a bus? Have you ever done that to a younger brother or sister?*

- *How do you think they felt? How would you feel if someone didn't make room for you?*

- *To be friendly and helpful and considerate and caring, just like the Girl Scout Law says, what should you do?*

Science Time: How Plants Drink

Page 9 of the girls' book shows how flowers take in water and food through their roots. Now's a great time to show the girls this process in action—and it's a lesson that will strengthen the girls' connection to the natural world.

Gather the girls around the slightly droopy plant that you've brought to the session. Invite a girl to water it.

Ask the girls to watch the plant for a few minutes. Ask: *Do you see any signs of the plant perking up?* If they do, ask: *How does it feel to see this plant "drink"? How do you feel when you drink some nice cool water when you're really thirsty? Do you think the plant feels the same way?*

Then ask: *How does it feel to learn something new?* (Answer: *Confident!*)

If nothing about the plant changes while the girls are watching, let them know that they can all check the plant later before they head home today.

Feast of Plant Parts

The picture on page 9 of the girls' book also introduces basic plant parts: flowers, stems, leaves, and roots. The girls might enjoy knowing that foods they eat represent all of these plant parts. Having a snack time feast of plant parts is a great way for the girls to match these parts (and also, of course, seeds) to foods that represent them (that's classifying!). Whether the feast is real or just visual (using photos or drawings), aim for foods local to your region to create a truly memorable experience for the girls! Here are some suggestions:

- **flowers:** broccoli and cauliflower florets
- **stems:** celery, asparagus, rhubarb
- **leaves:** lettuce, spinach, cabbage, kale
- **roots:** carrots, radishes, parsnip, turnips
- **seeds:** sunflower seeds, green beans

Then, if the girls didn't see the plant perk up after its "drink" of water, have them check on it. Ask: *Is it standing straight and tall or is it drooping at all?*

Role-Play: I'm Feeling This, You're Feeling That!

Ask the girls to team up in groups of four to try a role-play activity about feelings. Give them this scenario:

> *Three of you—Alexis, Jamaica, and Summer—are jumping rope outside Jamaica's house. Jamaica's next-door neighbor, Alisa, comes by and asks if she can play, too.*
>
> *Alexis doesn't want Alisa to join in the game. She says, "Alisa, your jacket is such an ugly color. It makes my eyes hurt. Go away."*
>
> *Jamaica and Summer can see that Alexis has made Alisa feel hurt.*

Then say: *Now, in your teams, decide which girl you will be and talk together about how to end this conflict. What will each of you say and do?*

Once the girls have figured out what they would do and say, have them present their solutions to the full group of Daisies. Then wrap up by guiding the Daisies through questions like these:

- *What do you think about what Alexis said to Alisa?*
- *Has anyone ever said anything like that to you? How did it make you feel?*
- *Have you ever said something like that? How do you think it made the other person feel?*
- *Why do you think it's good to be kind to all kinds of people?*
- *Why is it good to have different kinds of friends, and friends who like all kinds of things, even things you might not like? (Answer: Friends who are different from you let you learn new things—and meet new people!)*

Closing Ceremony: Earning the Blue Bucket Award

Ask the girls to come together in a Daisy Circle and tell one another what feelings they noticed today—in themselves and in their sister Daisies.

Then get a good discussion going that makes some points like these:

- *Our feelings can be different, from day to day and minute to minute.*
- *We might feel happy when we wake up in the morning but feel mad a short time later. And then something might make us laugh and we feel happy again. At other times, we might be bored, or nervous, or sad.*

- *Different things that happen to us can cause different feelings. Having different feelings for different things is good.*
- *What makes you happy might not make other people happy. And what makes you sad might not make other people sad.*
- *Knowing how other people around you feel helps you be a better friend.*
- *It's good to share our feelings with other people.*

Then, ask the girls:

- *What is the most important thing you've learned so far about feelings and talking about them—and getting along with others? Once we decide that, let's make a promise to teach that very important thing to others.*
- *Now let's go around our circle and say what we'd like to teach others.*

As each girl says what she thinks is most important, record it in your blue bucket on the next page. If the team has a blue bucket, invite the girls to toss their thoughts—symbolically or written on paper—into their bucket, too.

Then complete the closing ceremony by awarding the girls their Blue Bucket Award. Let them know that this award represents their learning some good thinking and talking skills, and agreeing to teach them to others. Encourage the Daisies to keep working on these skills, and to keep adding to their blue bucket all along the journey.

As the Daisies head home, encourage them to enjoy their book at home, and be sure to let them know that you look forward to your next time together.

Looking Ahead to Session 4

The Science Time in Session 4 shows girls how easily seeds can be scattered by wind or anything else that moves. This is first step to understanding why it's important to keep seeds where they belong. You and the Daisy Network might put together a nice collection of seeds, but inviting a gardener or farmer to visit with the girls and show them seeds lets you sit back and enjoy the fun and informative "seed blowing show"! Have on a hand a storage box and a fan (to simulate the wind)—even a tiny, hand-powered one will do!

The next session also features an origami activity of making butterflies. You might pull in a Network volunteer who enjoys origami, or perhaps there's an origami expert in your area! If so, she might inspire the girls to try a few other designs, too!

Blue Bucket of Words
OUR MOST IMPORTANT ONES!

SAMPLE SESSION 4
Living the Law, and So Many Seeds

In this Session, the girls will hear the first part of Chapter 2, where fireflies Lucy and Ace are on headlight duty.

You might like to know that Lucy and Ace are named for luciferin and luciferase, the two substances that help fireflies produce light.

Luciferin and *luciferase* are "big words," but little girls might find them funny, too. They're a good entry point to talking with the girls about their own names, what they mean, and why they were given them. If you have time to do this during today's gathering, great. If not, save the idea for another time.

AT A GLANCE

Goal: The girls explore living the Girl Scout Law through favorite flower friends and expand their knowledge of seeds and how they travel as a step to understanding how vegetation can vary around the world.

- Opening Ceremony: Have a Good Trip (Chinese) and Living the Law (Just Like a Flower Friend)

- Story Time

- Science Time: So Many Seeds

- A Walk in Nature to See Seeds

- Making Butterflies

- Closing Ceremony: How I "Lived" My Favorite Flower's Line of the Law

- Looking Ahead to Session 5

MATERIALS

- **Opening Ceremony:** crayons or markers to decorate luggage tags/bookmarks

- **Making Butterflies:** paper cut in squares (recycled wrapping paper can work well), enough to have 2 or 3 squares for each girl

PREPARE AHEAD

- Talk with any assistants about what they'll do before and during the session.

- Locate and invite a gardener or farmer to take part in the gathering by showing the girls a variety of seeds, especially seeds from your region.

- Practice making an origami butterfly so you can almost do it without thinking when you teach it to the girls. Advise any assistants or visitors to do the same. (Or substitute a craft activity you or a guest want to share with the girls that will also represent a beautiful outdoor critter that flies about *Between Earth and Sky*. Teen Girl Scouts may have lots of ideas that will go with this journey!)

AS GIRLS ARRIVE

Invite them to try the hidden pictures activity on page 21 of their book, where they have to find objects hidden amid all the shapes and colors. How many things can they find?

Opening Ceremony:
Have a Good Trip (Chinese)

Have the girls gather in a Daisy Circle. Let them know that today they will say "Have a great trip" to one another in Chinese, a language known by Gloria, the morning glory, who will soon appear in "A Road Trip to Remember."

In Chinese, "Have a good trip" is *Yi lu shun feng!* Going around the circle, ask each girl to say *Yi lu shun feng!* to the girl to her left. Once the girls have completed the circle, have them all say it together. Then invite them to add it to their luggage tag/bookmark!

Then invite all the girls to join together to say . . .

> *On my honor, I will try:*
> *To serve God and my country,*
> *To help people at all times,*
> *And to live by the Girl Scout Law.*

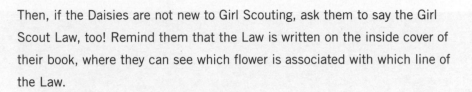

Then, if the Daisies are not new to Girl Scouting, ask them to say the Girl Scout Law, too! Remind them that the Law is written on the inside cover of their book, where they can see which flower is associated with which line of the Law.

Once they've said the Law, let them know they have a special job today:

● *Today, to honor the story of our flower friends, we are each going to pick our favorite flower and then agree to do one thing to show that we live the value of the Girl Scout Law that our flower lives.*

● *So, if Clover is your favorite flower, you're going to show how you use resources wisely. And if Sunny is your favorite, you'll find a way to be friendly and helpful.*

OK, let's go around our Daisy circle and each name our favorite flower friend and what she does to live the Girl Scout Law. And let's say what we will each do today to act like our favorite flower.

Story Time

Today, you'll be reading to the girls the first part of Chapter 2, where the flower friends travel to Maine, settle in at the Morning Glory Inn, and are served a breakfast of blueberry pancakes by Gloria. After you read to the girls (up to page 29, where Lupe says, "Wait and see"), get a discussion going with the Daisies by asking some questions like these:

● *In the story today, Lupe tells Clover that every place is special. What special places do you know? What makes them special?*

● *When the flower friends get to the Morning Glory Inn, they enjoy some blueberry pancakes. Do you like blueberry pancakes? Have you ever had them for breakfast?*

● *What did you eat for breakfast today? How did you feel afterward?*

● *What do you think makes a good breakfast that gives you a lot of energy for your day?*

Science Time: So Many Seeds

At their last gathering, the girls heard a section of the flower friends' story in which Zinni was worried about her seeds blowing around in the wind.

Gather the girls around the seeds that you or a visiting gardener or farmer have brought to show the girls. Encourage the girls to learn what the seeds are and to take time to see how they vary in size, shape, color, and texture.

Then place a bunch of the seeds in the box or other container you've brought in. Ideally the container will be fairly large and clear plastic, so all the girls can see inside it. Next, use the fan to simulate wind blowing the seeds about. If you have enough seeds and a good bit of "wind," the seeds will go flying about (maybe in a whirl), but will still stay within the confines of the box. Ask the girls:

- *Does this give you an idea of what lots of wind outdoors can do to seeds?*

- *Can you see how this can be a good way for seeds to spread themselves around?*

- *Can you think of times when having seeds blowing all over the place might not be good? When? What could happen that might not be good?*

Wrap up the discussion by asking: *Can you see how if we are all careful with seeds, we are helping to take good care of Planet Earth?*

A Walk in Nature to See Seeds

This outdoor time gives the Daisies an opportunity to enjoy all the wonders of nature while getting a firsthand look, depending on your location and the time of year, at the variety of seeds that fall to the ground in parks or wooded areas. Before heading out, have the girls take a look at the "SEEDS . . . " page of their book (page 36). Explain to them the information on that page (depending on how you structure your outing, you might also talk with the Daisies about weeds, using the information on page 37):

SEEDS
- are baby plants just waiting to grow.
- can be blown by the wind or carried by animals or water.
- can stick to clothes and shoes, too. These are the ways seeds travel far from home. Weeds are plants that grow where they're not wanted.

Once the girls are outside, get them searching. You might say:

- *Let's see who finds the most kinds of seeds fallen to the ground.*

- *How many sizes, shapes, colors, and textures of seeds can you find? Let's start looking!*

SCIENCE IN PLAY!

Observing, communicating, and classifying—the girls are practicing basic science skills once again!

DON'T FORGET TO LEAVE NO TRACE

Whenever you venture outdoors with the Daisies, be sure to remind them of Leave No Trace practices. They can pick up nature items that have fallen to the ground but they should not pick, pluck, or otherwise disturb living things.

Making Butterflies

Origami is the Japanese art of paper folding. Some of its creations, like the butterfly described below, are definitely simple enough for young girls to make. The butterfly is also a good critter for this journey—it's a traveler between earth and sky. So these paper butterflies will make a nice keepsake—a reminder of the beautiful things found in nature.

Keep in mind that the girls may not listen to the exact origami directions. They may just go off on their own and create their own folded paper creation. That's part of the fun or origami!

How to Make a Butterfly in Four Folds

Start with a square of paper that's at least 6 inches by 6 inches. If the paper has a pattern, put the pattern side down.

Fold the paper in half along the diagonal to create a triangle.

Then fold the triangle in half to create a smaller triangle.

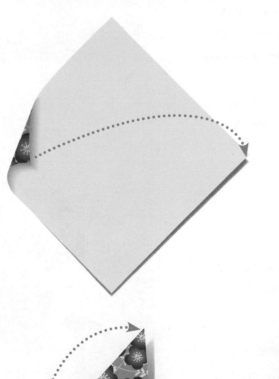
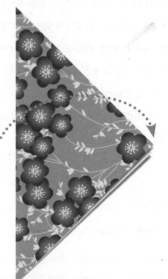

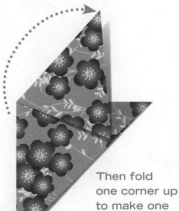
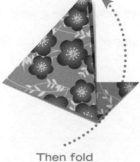

Then fold one corner up to make one butterfly wing.

Then fold the second wing up.

Open the butterfly and you're done! Press gently on the "body" to make the wings flap!

66

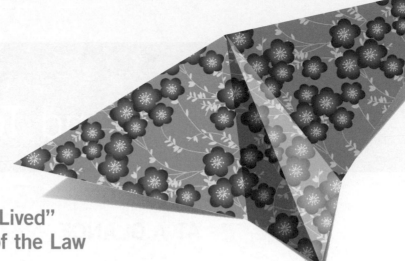

Closing Ceremony: How I "Lived" My Favorite Flower's Line of the Law

Ask the girls to come together again in a Daisy Circle so they can each say the name of their favorite flower friend and what they did today to "live" the line of the Girl Scout Law that flower stands for.

You might start off by saying:

- *Lupe is my favorite flower friend. She's honest and fair, just like the third line of the Girl Scout Law.*

- *To be honest and fair today, I gave everyone three pieces of paper to make butterflies. That was all the paper I had, and it let everyone have an equal share. That's being fair!*

After all the girls have a had a chance to name their favorite flower and what they did to "live" her today, complete the closing ceremony with the girls reciting as much of the Law as they can. Then invite them to close out their gathering with a friendship squeeze!

Encourage the girls to enjoy their book between sessions, especially pages 27 and 28, which ask the girls to name local fruits and favorite places. Let the Daisies know that you look forward to the group's next time together.

Looking Ahead to Session 5

The Science Time in the next session has the girls exploring how the colors of stones get brighter when wet. You and the Daisy Friends and Family Network may be able to gather a variety of stones on your own—especially if you live in a region famous for rock hounding, or one known for lapidary artists. Or you might invite a rock hound or lapidary artist to visit with the girls. Then you can sit back and enjoy the fun and informative "Stone Light, Stone Bright" show, too!

SAMPLE SESSION 5
Special Skills, and Textures, Too

AT A GLANCE

Goal: Girls continue to explore their similarities and differences as they consider the skills they contribute to their Daisy group and gain an understanding of the diversity of textures in nature.

- Opening Ceremony: Have a Good Trip (Japan) and Paying Attention to Our Skills

- Story Time

- Science Time: Stone Light, Stone Bright

- A Walk in Nature to Find Shapes

- Closing Ceremony: I Think Your Special Skill Is . . .

- Looking Ahead to Session 6

MATERIALS

- **As Girls Arrive:** an old suitcase, briefcase, box, or other container that the girls can decorate to hold all their "skills"; crayons, markers, decorative bits

- **Stone Light, Stone Bright:** an array of stones in many colors and bowls of

  water to dip them in

- **Walk in Nature to Find Shapes:** If the girls can't venture outdoors, have an array of natural objects on hand representing various shapes (see page 71)

PREPARE AHEAD

Talk with any assistants about what they'll do before and during the session.

AS GIRLS ARRIVE

Fireflies light the way in the road trip story with their special light-producing skills. The Daisies have special skills, too! Invite them to decorate the firefly suitcase that will hold all their special skills. The suitcase is another fun container for their journey, just like their blue bucket.

Opening Ceremony: Have a Good Trip (Japan) and Paying Attention to Our Skills

Have the girls gather in a Daisy Circle. Let them know that today they will say "Have a great trip" to one another in Japanese, a language that Clover probably knows, because she's from all over the world.

In Japanese, have a good trip is *Itterasshai!* Going around the circle, ask each girl to say *Itterasshai!* to the girl to her left. Once the girls have completed the circle, have them all say it together. Then invite them to add this new word to their luggage tags/bookmarks.

Next, let them know they have a new special job today. Say something like:

- *During our Daisy time together today, you are all going to pay careful attention to the girl who's now on your left. Does everyone know which way is left?*

- *Pay attention to what she says and does so that you can learn what special skill she shows during our gathering today. Is she good at speaking up? Good at helping others?*

- *At the end of our gathering, you'll tell her what you think her special skill is and she'll let you know if she agrees with you or not!*

Keep in mind that the skills the Daisies notice and then choose to develop will step them through to earning their Firefly Award, which is named for the fireflies Lucy and Ace, who use their special skill of making light to light the way for the flower friends on their road trip.

Story Time

Today, you'll be reading to the girls the final pages of Chapter 2, where the flower friends visit Jasper Beach before heading to the Lupine Festival. After you (or a guest) read the story to the girls, get a discussion going by asking some questions like these:

- *What did you think about the flowers seeing so many colors and shapes at a beach?*

- *Have you ever been to a beach like that?*

- *Can you imagine going to a beach like that?*

Learning about the many wonders of nature helps the girls develop an appreciation for the environment—and a desire to protect it.

This discussion leads nicely into today's "Science Time" activity, so go to it!

Science Time: Stone Light, Stone Bright!

Invite the Daisies to experiment with the array of stones and the bowls of water that you or any guests have set out.

You might say: *Here's a way to see some shiny stones and pebbles, just like the flower friends saw when they visited Jasper Beach.*

You might ask: *Why do you think water makes your stone brighter?*

Depending on what the girls answer, you might explain that when stones get wet, the water on them acts like a mirror:

- *The water lets more light reflect off the stone.*

- *More light means you can see more of the stone's color. So the stone looks brighter.*

- *Over time, water and sand can make stones so smooth and shiny they look polished—that's what the flowers were seeing at Jasper Beach.*

OBSERVING!

Science skills are in play once again as the girls take a close look at the differences between wet stones and dry stones!

A Walk in Nature to Find Shapes

Just as the flower friends enjoy all the shapes and colors in nature, so too can the Daisies! Before heading outdoors for a walk focused on finding beautiful shapes in nature, ask the girls to name some of the shapes they know.

If you have a whiteboard or chalkboard, invite each girl to draw a favorite shape on the board. Or you might use newsprint on an easel or smaller sheets of paper so that each girl has her own "list" of shapes. Aim for a well-rounded list of basic shapes, such as circles, squares, triangles, and stars. If the girls know more shapes—diamonds, hearts, ovals, rectangles, spirals—by all means, add them in!

Explain that the girls will now take a walk outdoors, where they'll try to find objects that match all the shapes they've just named.

As the girls walk, have them share what they find. When they're back indoors, get a discussion going with questions like these:

- *How many shapes did you find from our list? Which couldn't you find?*
- *Did the shapes you found outside surprise you at all?*
- *Did you find any shapes that you'd never seen before or didn't know the name of?*
- *Where else might we look for shapes outdoors? Do you think we could find places with even more shapes? Where?*

RIGHT, LEFT, EAST, WEST

Whenever you can, add a little travel lesson on directions into your gatherings with the Daisies.

If you can easily point them east or west based on the sun's location, you can teach them some simple direction basics, such as:

- If you're facing east, north will be to your left and south will be to your right.
- If you're facing west, north will be to your right and south will be to your left.
- If you're facing north, east will be to your right, and south will be to your left.

You might see if the girls can figure out the location of east, west, and north if they are facing south.

You can even experiment with a simple compass and show the girls how to get the compass to point north. Then see if they can locate the other three directions.

HOW DID IT FEEL TO BE OUTDOORS?

When the Daisies return from their romp in nature, be sure to ask them:

How did it feel to out and about in the fresh air Between Earth and Sky?

See if the girls can come up with some new feeling words to add to their blue bucket!

Closing Ceremony: I Think Your Special Skill Is . . .

Ask the girls to form a Daisy Circle, in the same order they were at their opening ceremony. Then go around the circle and ask each girl to name the special skill that she noticed today in the girl to her left.

A girl might say something like, "I think Annie is good at paying attention to how others are feeling because she helped out Nina and Alexis today and they didn't even ask for help." Then Annie can say whether she thinks paying attention to how others are feeling is a skill of hers or she has another skill that she thinks is even better.

As the girls name one another's skills, keep track of them on the next page of this guide. Help the Daisies keep a list of them, too—either in their suitcase or in a list like yours. How many skills have the girls named? How many skills do they share? What other skills can they name that no one has mentioned yet? What skills do they want to get better at on this journey?

After a good discussion, complete the closing ceremony with friendship squeeze. Encourage the girls to enjoy their book between sessions, and be sure to let the Daisies know that you look forward to the group's next Girl Scout time together.

Looking Ahead to Session 6

The next session's Story Time focuses on Chapter 3, where Sunny the sunflower is helping clean soil in Pittsburgh so more gardens can grow. This session would be an ideal time to invite a visitor who uses plants to clean the soil or the air, or one who can introduce the girls to various plants that clean the soil or the air. Check in with gardeners in your area and with any community garden programs. A visitor in the know can even show the Daisies a place where the soil is being cleaned or has been cleaned—so a field trip may be in order. Or perhaps the girls can visit a building in the community that is taking advantage of greenery to keep the air clean.

As always, if a visitor or a field trip isn't possible, you might instead share photos of soil- and air-cleaning plants with the girls, and also areas being cleaned by plants. These might include photos of green roofs, which not only clean the air but help lower hot summer temperatures.

Daisies' Skills for the Road

We Have Skills and So Do Plants

AT A GLANCE

Goal: The girls make use of their special skills and begin to understand the special skills of plants, too.

- Opening Ceremony: Have a Good Trip (Italian) and Making the Most of Our Special Skills

- Story Time

- Option: Science Time and a Nature Walk, Too

- Option: Cooking Up Some Color

- Closing Ceremony: Our Special Skills

- Looking Ahead to Session 7

MATERIALS

- **Opening Ceremony:** art supplies for decorating the girls' luggage tags/ bookmarks

- **Cooking Up Some Color (Optional):** Natural paints, muffin tins, brushes, and paper; or fruits, vegetables, and other equipment as needed for making the paints with the girls

PREPARE AHEAD

Talk with any assistants about what they'll do before and during the session.

AS GIRLS ARRIVE

Invite them to continue decorating their firefly suitcase, or they may want to add to their journey poster.

Opening Ceremony: Have a Good Trip and Making the Most of Our Special Skills

Have the girls gather in a Daisy Circle. Let them know that today they will say "Have a great trip" to one another in Italian, a language that Lupe and Clover probably know, because they both have family all over the world.

In Italian, have a good trip is *Buon viaggio!* Going around the circle, ask each girl to say *Buon viaggio!* to the girl to her left. Once the girls have completed the circle, have them all say it together. Then invite them to add this new phrase to their luggage tags/bookmarks.

Next, let them know they have a new special job today. Say something like:

- *During our last Daisy time together, we paid attention to a sister Daisy's special skills. Today we'll pay attention to our own skills.*

- *Choose a skill that you will use today.*

- *Let's go around our circle and each say a special skill we're going to use.*

- *At the end of our time together today, we'll all talk about how our special skills worked out for today.*

Story Time

In Chapter 3 of the story, Lupe and Clover start off talking about their feelings and then the flower friends meet up with Sunny, the Sunflower, who is helping clean the soil in Pittsburgh. After you (or a guest) read the story to the girls, get a discussion going about how considerate Clover was to talk with Lupe—and how honest Lupe was in her answer.

You might ask: *What if Clover hadn't said anything? What if Lupe hadn't said that everything was OK?*

Then move on to talk about Sunny's special skill—cleaning the soil. Most people probably don't know that sunflowers can clean poisons from the soil. But perhaps your region is using sunflowers or other plants to clean the soil or the air. If so, you and the Daisies can see these plants in action firsthand.

OPTION: SCIENCE TIME AND A NATURE WALK, TOO

This discussion and any outdoor excursion you and the Daisies make to see plants at work cleaning the soil or air will make a nice segue to the girls thinking again about their own special skills.

OPTION: COOKING UP SOME COLOR

If the Daisies have time in this gathering, enjoy some fun with natural paints made from foods. Here's a sampling of food/color pairings that you and some assistants might create ahead of time and have on hand for the girls:

- beets for red
- carrots for orange
- grass or spinach for green
- berries (raspberries, blueberries, cranberries) for blues, purples, red and pink

Just place your chosen colorful ingredient in a pot of water (twice the amount of water than the vegetables or plants), bring the water to a boil, and simmer for 30 minutes to one hour.

Once the water is a bright color, let it cool and place it in muffin tins so the girls can dip their brushes and test out the "paint." Be sure to step the girls through the paint-making process if they didn't see it firsthand.

Also, sometimes fresh beets are so intense in color that you and the girls might experiment with taking chunks of cut beets and letting them sit in a small amount of water to create pink "paint."

Frozen berries can be thawed and strained to achieve richly colored water. You might also experiment with nuts and onion skins to create browns and tans.

Closing Ceremony: Our Special Skills

Ask the girls to come together again in a Daisy Circle. Then invite the girls to take turns saying the special skill they tried out today and how it went.

As the girls name their skills, add them to the suitcase on page 77.

Now, get the girls talking about how they might continue to use these special skills. Ask:

- *What can you do at home to make even more use of this skill of yours?*
- *How about at school?*
- *Is there any way for you to use this skill in your neighborhood, too?*

After a good discussion, complete the closing ceremony by giving the Daisies their Firefly Award. Let them know that it represents their having a special skill that they can use to help others and the planet. Then end the ceremony with a friendship squeeze.

Looking Ahead to Session 7

The next session offers extended time to focus on Chapter 4 of the flower friends' story, which takes place in Wisconsin and Utah. This is an ideal time for the team to enjoy a special snack time featuring your region's local foods—a parallel to the flower friends enjoying the milk and cheese of Dairyland—and to enjoy a local national treasure, just as the flower friends enjoy Utah's Great Salt Lake.

If cheese is made in your area (and none of the girls have milk allergies), great—but any local food will work well for a snack. If you live in apple country, for example, arrange for the girls to sample several varieties of apples—and various ways of serving them, such as fresh, baked, and dried.

With your Network, seek out local growers and producers. A few might agree to visit with the girls and bring samples of their foods.

As for a local, natural treasure, think ahead about various places to share with the girls. You'll be asking them where the flower friends might go if they visited your hometown, so be ready with some great places if the girls need help coming up with one.

More Daisies' Skills for the Road

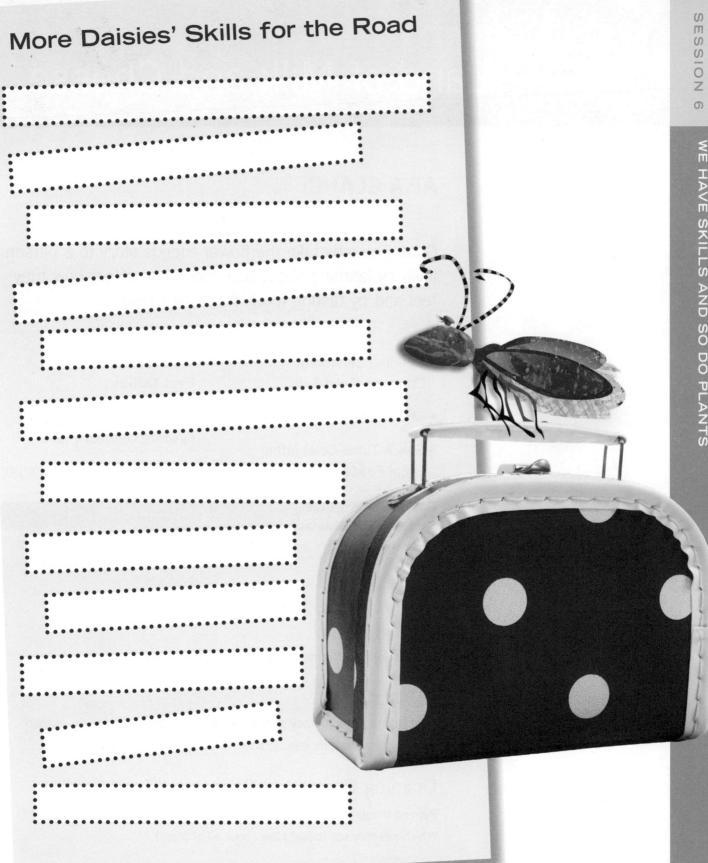

In the Land of Milk and Cheese

AT A GLANCE

Goal: The girls take the flower friends story to a personal level by learning about how foods can affect how they feel and by tasting foods from their region.

- Opening Ceremony: Choose a Good Trip

- Story Time

- Snack Time: Celebrating Local Foods

- A Walk in Nature to Find Textures

- Closing Ceremony: My Favorite Outdoor Place

- Looking Ahead to Session 8

MATERIALS

- **Story Time:** the girls' book and this guide

- **Snack Time:** any local foods you or invited guests plan to serve and talk about with the girls

PREPARE AHEAD

Talk with any assistants about their roles before and during the session.

AS GIRLS ARRIVE

Take out the team journey poster the girls have been working on. Is there anything else the girls want to add?

Opening Ceremony: Choose a "Good Trip"

Remind the girls of all the ways they've learned to say "Have a good trip!" Which will they say today? How about all of them?

Story Time

Today, the girls will enjoy Chapter 4 of the road trip story, in which the flower friends enjoy a stop in Wisconsin's Dairyland, taste a lot of cheese, and then have a picnic before heading to the Great Salt Lake. Before reading past page 54, where Lupe takes a nap, ask the girls if they know why all the cheese and milk made Lupe sleepy.

If no one knows why, give them the scoop on "sleeper" foods by saying something like this:

> *Did you know that some foods, like milk and cheese, can help you sleep? You can think of some foods as sleeper foods and some foods as wake-up foods—because some foods calm us down enough to get a good night's rest and other foods rev up our energy. What foods get you all revved up?*

This discussion also makes a nice lead-in to the special Snack Time of the girls sampling a selection of cheeses—or other local foods from your region.

JUST SO YOU KNOW!

Milk and cheese are among the various foods that make people sleepy. It's no wonder people often recommend drinking a warm glass of milk at bedtime!

If you're wondering, yes, these foods are high in tryptophan. The body uses tryptophan to make serotonin, which helps regulate sleep.

Cheese and milk have more tryptophan than turkey, the holiday favorite that is often thought of as a sleep-inducer.

Continue reading to the girls the rest of Chapter 4 and then get them thinking about what places in their region might be special, just like the Great Salt Lake that the flower friends visit. You might ask:

- *If the flowers were to visit our town, what would they want to see?*

- *What would be the best thing to show them?*

- *What foods would they want to try?*

- *When they visited this special place in our town, would they see any special skills at work—people skills or plant skills?*

Snack Time: Celebrating Local Foods

Now's the time for the girls to sample local foods, and to hear from any invited guests who will talk with them about what's made in your region.

A Walk in Nature to Find Textures

This outdoor time gives the Daisies an opportunity to enjoy all the wonders of nature while expanding their knowledge of textures. Before heading out, talk to the girls about how different things are smooth, rough, soft, or hard, depending on what they are and what they are made of. You might say:

> *A sweater is soft, but a table is hard. A stone may be smooth, but tree bark can be rough. Some cheeses are very soft and some are hard!*

Let the girls know that how something feels is called its texture. Ask each girl to take a turn naming a texture. If you have a room filled with a variety of items, have the girls choose something in the room that shows their favorite texture so that all the girls can feel it.

Make a master list of all the textures the girls name so that you can take it with you when you and the girls head outdoors. Aim for a well-rounded list of textures. If the textures the girls named don't create a very diverse list, add in some textures of your own and explain each one in turn to the Daisies.

The aim of the short romp in nature today is for the girls to find as many textures in nature as they can. In finding the textures, the girls won't need to remove anything from nature. Be sure to emphasize this.

It would be great if the girls could draw each texture they find, by drawing the item. So pass out some paper and crayons and head outdoors! Below is a list of textures the girls might focus on. You might call them out one by one, moving forward to the next texture once all the girls have found the one you've named. Just say: *OK, now let's all find something . . .*

- *soft*
- *rough*
- *hard*
- *pointy*
- *rounded*
- *that goes "crunch"*
- *that goes "swoosh"*
- *smooth*
- *shiny*
- *glossy*

Closing Ceremony: My Favorite Outdoor Place

Gather the girls together in a Daisy Circle and ask them to name their favorite outdoor place. Prompt them to keep in mind colors, shapes, textures, and smells—everything they've been noticing on this journey.

To get the girls going, you might give them this sentence to finish:

> *My favorite outdoor place I've ever been is* _____ .

If they're up for it, ask them to fill in this sentence, too:

> *I feel* _____ *when I'm there.*

This closing ceremony helps set the pace for choosing a Clover project. Keep track of all the special places the Daisies name. They might just include a great place for the group's upcoming project.

HOW DID IT FEEL TO BE OUTDOORS?

When the Daisies return from their romp in nature, continue the tradition! Ask:

How did it feel to be out and about in the fresh air Between Earth and Sky?

See if the girls can come up with some new feeling words to add to their blue bucket! You might ask: *Do any of your feelings match up to the textures you found today? For example, I felt very smooth walking around outdoors! How did you feel?*

Add the Daisies' words to your bucket—the big one for the girls and one of the buckets in this guide, too!

A GREAT CLOVER PROJECT

- allows girls to use their special skills—words and deeds—to protect Earth's resources

- relies on girl input in choosing and planning

- gives girls the opportunity to work as a team

- enables girls to advocate for taking care of nature by talking to others and educating and inspiring them—Daisy-style!

PROJECT EXAMPLES

- Partner with a school library or other community building to make posters encouraging people to mind their seeds and weeds

- Host a family meeting to ask all families to mind their seeds and weeds

- Make a booklet, play, or other creative endeavor to offer tips for protecting local vegetation to other girls, families, or schools

- learn about a local bird or critter that needs protecting and create a simple way to spread the word!

- Work with local officials to find ways to add local plants to urban spaces, such as median strips and sidewalk borders

- Check with local officials to see if city lots can be cleaned and then planted—a la Sunny, the sunflower, and her work in Pittsburgh!

- Something else based on the girls' imaginations!

Looking Ahead to Session 8

The Daisies will try some bark rubbings during the next gathering, so get with your Network and select a good location for getting close to trees!

THINKING AHEAD TO A GREAT CLOVER PROJECT

Now is also a good time for you and your Network to think ahead about how to guide the Daisies to use their special skills—their words and deeds— toward their Clover Award. Is there a local treasure the girls could work to preserve and protect? Is there a patch of land they might clear of unwanted vegetation? Did an idea emerge from the closing ceremony of Session 7? Do they want to have an all-out weed pull and invite community members to join them? Or do they want to take the project in another resource-saving direction?

Review the Project Examples to the left and then get together with your Daisy Network to plot out some possibilities for the girls to consider, using the chart on the next page. Get ready to guide the girls to a great Clover project!

Possible Projects	What This Will Do for Earth	What Daisies Will Have an Opportunity to Learn, Say, and Do

How Big A Project?

NOT MUCH TIME?

Guide the team toward an imaginative way of caring for a natural treasure that does not require a lot of advance preparation. What matters is that the girls have a chance to share what they've learned and then invite others to join in with them, too.

PLENTY OF TIME?

If the Daisies can add a few sessions to the journey (and have enough helpers!), they might go all out with a weed pull or planting session. The team could make invitations to their event, plan some earthy refreshments to serve, and make a great Daisy time of it.

SAMPLE SESSION 8
When the Flowers Meet the Trees

AT A GLANCE

Goal: The Daisies choose a project idea, practice talking about it, and create visual tools for their project.

- **Opening Ceremony:** Favorite Trees
- **Story Time**
- **Snack Time: Hot Drinks and Cool Drinks**
- **Option: A Walk in Nature to Rub a Tree**
- **Closing Ceremony: What We're Doing and Why**
- **Looking Ahead to Session 9**

MATERIALS

- **Story Time:** the girls' book and this guide
- **Snack Time: Hot Drinks and Cool Drinks:** Enough tea or fruit drinks,

  hot and cold to serve the Daisies
- **A Walk in Nature to Rub a Tree:** construction paper, crayons, and masking tape

PREPARE AHEAD

With your Daisy Network, select a location for the bark rubbings and arrange any needed transportation and additional volunteers.

AS GIRLS ARRIVE

Invite girls to add more details to their team journey poster.

Opening Ceremony: Favorite Trees

Invite the girls into a friendship circle and, in honor of the chestnut tree they will hear about in today's Story Time, invite them each to name their favorite tree. They might choose to say their favorite kind of tree or simply a favorite tree and where it lives. Anything goes!

Story Time

Today, the girls will enjoy Chapter 5 of the road trip story, in which the flower friends travel through the hot desert, bump into Tatiana, the tumbleweed, enjoy some cool shakes, and then meet up with Jaz, the jasmine. From Jaz, they learn the story of another "comeback" tree, the chestnut.

Remind the Daisies that this is the third tree they've learned about on this journey: *First we learned about spruce trees, then piñon pines, and now chestnut trees. And we have one more tree to learn about later in the story! Can anyone guess what it will be?*

Get a discussion going about the trees in your region and what the Daisies like about them. You might ask:

- *Which trees give us shade?*
- *Which ones are good for climbing?*
- *Which ones grow near you?*

The girls might enjoy knowing that Juliette "Daisy" Gordon Low, the founder of Girl Scouts, enjoyed climbing trees as a young girl. As one of her cousins, Caroline Stiles Lovell, wrote:

> "We lived in trees, and in the big old ivy tree on the grass each of us had her special room. The orchard, too, was familiar ground, and, from the first ripe cherries to the last mealy pears, we climbed the trees and feasted . . . "

> —From "Twenty Cousins in the Summer-Time—and Daisy Low One of the Cousins"
> by Caroline Stiles Lovell, in *Juliette and the Girl Scouts*,
> edited by Anne Hyde Choate and Helen Ferris (Girl Scouts, 1928)

Snack Time: Hot Drinks and Cool Drinks

In honor of the flower friends' desert adventure, you might serve hot tea and cool tea to the girls. You can even make this Snack Time into a little science experiment. If it's a hot day, which drink cools the girls faster? If it's a cold day, is it too cold for iced tea?

BARKING UP SOME LOVELY TREES!

Tree trunks are the oldest part of a tree, so their bark is often rougher than the bark on limbs and smaller branches. Some bark is brown, some is white, some is silvery. The bark of a sycamore tree, which varies from light to dark in big patches, looks like a partly finished jigsaw puzzle!

What kinds of trees—and what kinds of bark—can you show the Daisies?

Option: A Walk in Nature to Rub a Tree

If the girls can get out for another short jaunt in nature, this is a good time to make some bark rubbings. Tree bark comes in all sorts of colors and textures, from silver to brown and from smooth to thick and rough. It all depends on the variety of tree.

Here's how to get started: You'll need a piece of construction paper for each girl or pair of girls, and a roll of masking tape and crayons.

Once outside, ask the girls to find some trees with interesting bark. Then have them tape their paper to the bark and rub over the paper in up and down strokes with a crayon until they get an interesting pattern. Encourage the girls to try several trees so their paper has a variety of rubbings on it.

When the girls are done, bring them together for a discussion. You might ask: *What kind of patterns do you see? Can you see any shapes within the patterns?*

MISTAKES? NO PROBLEM!

Mistakes are a great way for girls to learn. And often they result in something truly creative!

If the Daisies feel they "messed up" their bark rubbings, invite them to talk about what went wrong (Did the paper fall off the tree? Did it rip while being rubbed?) and what they might do differently next time now that they've learned this new art form!

Getting Ready for the Clover Project

Based on the ideas gathering in Session 7, and your conversations with the Daisy Friends and Family Network, let the girls know what the Clover project is that they will be teaming up on for their next gathering.

Encourage the Daisies to give some simple Girl Led input:

- What will they bring?
- What skills will they be packing?
- What supplies will they pack?
- What will they each do?
- What will they say? Ask?

OPTION: CREATIVE PROJECT MESSAGES

The Daisies may enjoy making posters and other simple messages for their project, depending on the nature of the treasure they are protecting and what's needed.

Creating project posters and other messages is another great way for the girls to practice communication skills.

Closing Ceremony: What We're Doing and Why

Now that the girls have in mind what they're going to do for their Clover project, use this closing ceremony to coach them toward simple ways to explain what they're doing and why it matters.

Gather the girls in a Daisy Circle and ask them to each come up with a way to end these sentences:

> *Our Daisy group is doing a project to _____.*

> *It's important because _____ .*

Encourage the girls to share this information with family and friends, and even their teachers. The more people the girls talk to, the more people they might inspire to join in on the project.

Looking Ahead to Session 9

This next session is the time for the Daisies to do their Clover project. The nature of the project will determine the location and timing of the session and any extras the girls enjoy.

You and the girls can decide whether to enjoy the final chapter of the road trip story during the Clover project outing or save it for a later time. If you save it for later, you might consider adding in a full story session to celebrate this final chapter (see below).

OPTION: SPECIAL CLOVER GATHERING

You may want to add in a session or two, including a special gathering of the Daisy Friends and Family Network to talk about the Clover project and read Chapter 5 of the flower friends' story.

Protecting a Natural Treasure

AT A GLANCE

Goal: The Daisies team up to protect a natural treasure of Earth and carry out their Clover project.

- Opening Ceremony: How We're Feeling
- Story Time
- Clover Project
- Closing Ceremony
- Looking Ahead to Session 10

MATERIALS

- **Story Time:** the girls' book and this guide
- Any supplies or materials needed for the Clover project

PREPARE AHEAD

Reach out to the Daisy Friends and Family Network to ensure that there are enough rides and helpers available for the Clover project day.

Talk to those in charge of wherever the project is taking place to review any logistics. Based on your team's plan, pave the way for the Daisies' effort!

Options: For some extra fun, girls might also like to spend some group time on activities in their *Between Earth and Sky* book, including "Seeds, Nuts, Fruits, and Cones" on page 92, which asks the girls to identify seeds and nuts that they've learned about along the journey.

AS GIRLS ARRIVE

Remind them that they are gathering today to have an opportunity to be like flower friend Clover: They will use resources wisely to protect a local treasure—and that's a way to help Planet Earth.

Opening Ceremony: How We're Feeling

Gather the girls in a Daisy Circle and invite them to say how they feel about the Clover project they are about to do. To get them started, give them these lines to finish with their own thoughts:

Today we are teaming up to protect what needs protecting. I feel

_____ about that!

Story Time

As the flower friends' road trip story reaches its final chapter, what the Daisies hear about White Sweetclover in Alaska is really the story of an invasive plant in North America's last frontier.

Invasive plants basically hitch-hiked into Alaska in cars, planes, ships, and on tires and the soles of shoes. Some even cropped up in potted plants at national chain stores. (That's how Lori Zaumseil, profiled on page 91 of the girls' book, met her first invasive species!)

So you and the Daisies might think of invasive plants as pioneers—they're hardy and they know how to outsmart, and outlive, the natives. They can grow taller than the local plants (remember Yellow Lupine?) so they block the sun from reaching them. Basically, they're a tough bunch!

After the girls finish hearing the story, get a discussion going by asking:

> If you had to rewrite this section of the story so it happened right where we live, what plants and flowers would be in it? What would they do and say?

The girls might like to draw their own "local" version. If so, get out the crayons and paper.

Clover Project

Get to it! Engage the girls and their families in the Clover project they've chosen. And feel good about doing something for Daisies and for Earth!

Closing Ceremony

After work on the Clover project is complete, gather the Daisies together for a quick closing ceremony. Let them know how proud you are of their efforts to protect a natural treasure. Then invite the girls to say how proud they are of each other, too!

Looking Ahead to Session 10

Get together with the Daisy Friends and Family Network to create a Daisy-worthy final celebration to this journey.

Be sure to get the girls' thoughts and ideas, too. You might ask:

- *What guests might you like to invite?*
- *Do you want to create thank-you notes for all the special visitors you've met on this journey?*

PRIDE = SELF-CONFIDENCE

Letting the girls know the value of their project and the quality of their work builds their confidence and encourages them to keep going—now and on future efforts, whether for the environment or anything else!

- *What songs might you like to sing?*

- *Do you want to display your blue bucket and your firefly suitcase?*

- *How about the team's cut-paper journey poster?*

- *What else might you like to do?*

- *What treats do you want to serve?*

Also take a look at the suggestions on pages 94 and 95 and use them as you like to create the best possible celebration for your group of girls.

SAMPLE SESSION 10
On the Road to New Adventures

AT A GLANCE

Goal: The Daisies celebrate all they've learned and done along the journey!

- Opening Ceremony: It's the Law!
- Words and Deeds
- Clover Award Ceremony
- Celebrate with Shapes and Colors
- Imagining What Happens Next

MATERIALS

- Any items or materials needed for the celebration, including the girls' blue bucket, firefly suitcase, and cut-paper journey poster

PREPARE AHEAD

Think back on all the Daisies have accomplished—in terms of communicating their feelings, learning about the environment, and taking part in the science skills of observing, communicating, and classifying. Be ready to remind them of how they succeeded. If possible, plan to display some visuals of the girls adventures over the course of the journey.

AS GIRLS ARRIVE

Remind them that today they have guests arriving. Encourage them to greet their guests and take turns sharing the details of their team journey poster, their blue bucket, their suitcase of skills, and any other journey items they've chosen to display.

Opening Ceremony: It's the Law!

Invite the girls to form an inner circle as the guests they will educate and inspire form an outer circle around them. (Perhaps a Daisy can give these instructions and teach the guests the Girl Scout Quiet Sign, too!)

Ask the girls to say the Girl Scout Promise. Now ask them to repeat it, but this time, the outer circle needs to say it with them, loudly and with energy! (They can read it on the inside cover of their book or from a larger version you may have posted.)

Now ask the girls to make a circle around their Daisy garden picture and invite them to each say one way they lived some of the values that the flower friends represent. Remind them that they can look at the Law on the inside front cover of their book, which also shows all the flowers.

"Using resources wisely" may be mentioned right away! Encourage girls to reflect on other ways they have lived the Law, too. Offer the girls a few prompts to remind them of all their accomplishments.

- Perhaps they have been a sister to other Girl Scouts.

- They may have been considerate and caring, or friendly and helpful.

- Or maybe they were responsible for what they say and do (by following up on their plans).

QUIET PLEASE!

If you haven't already taught the Daisies the Quiet Sign, let them know that it's simply holding up a hand with all five fingers extended. It is based on what used to be known as the Fifth Law—A Girl Scout is courteous. The 1928 book *Scouting for Girls* notes, "True courtesy is a sign of real consideration for the rights of others." Later Girl Scout handbooks noted, "Courtesy is more than saying 'thank you' and 'excuse me.' It is consideration for others, although their ideas, ways of living, and beliefs may differ from [your] own."

Now, which flower friend is considerate and caring?

Words and Deeds

Let the girls know that the right words and deeds are what leadership is all about. Then invite them to take turns showing their favorite words and deeds from their blue bucket and firefly suitcase. They can choose their own contributions or those of a friend.

Then ask the girls to pair up and give each pair a spot to sit in. Ask each girl to remember a way her partner used her skills or feelings on this journey. Encourage the partners to share their thoughts with each other.

Then give each girl a piece of paper so she can draw a picture of one way in which her partner showed her special skill. Have helpers assist the girls with adding a word or two to their pictures.

Gather the team together again and have each girl say how her partner used her special skill on this journey. Then have the partners give their drawings to each other as a gift—and a keepsake for their *Between Earth and Sky* book.

Clover Award Ceremony

To get started, give the girls a chance to say how they feel about their Clover project. Be sure to let them know what you believe they accomplished on behalf of their local natural treasure. Give them examples of the teamwork you saw in action, too!

Ask: *Would you like to give yourselves a round of applause? Or do you have another special Daisy way to celebrate this journey together?*

Now present each girl with her Clover Award and invite her to say in her own words how she feels about completing this journey. You might offer the girls one of the following statements to complete as they consider what to say:

- *The most important thing I learned during our Clover project is . . .*
- *I am proud of our project because we . . .*
- *I think our project is important because . . .*

And then . . .

. . . Celebrate with Shapes and Colors!

How about an array of healthful snacks in all shapes and colors? Consider fruits and cheeses cut into an array of shapes with cookie cutters. Let the Daisies do the cutting!

And don't forget candied fruit pops, like those of chef Amanda Cohen (profiled on page 93 of the girls' book).

Add in some favorite songs about travel, too! How about some road songs? "On the Road Again," anyone? Or check out the lyrics to that old Girl Scout favorite, "Barges."

And how about photos and autographs? A team photo around the cut-paper journey poster would make a nice memento for the girls. So would autographs. Perhaps the girls would like to sign one another's books and add a little doodle, too!

Imagining What Happens Next

If the Daisy Team will continue on with other Girl Scout adventures this year, spend a few minutes at the conclusion of the celebration getting the girls excited about what's to come.

If the girls will be Brownies next year, get them thinking of a special farewell celebration to give their flower friends (but remind them that the flowers will always be there whenever they say the Girl Scout Law!). After all, flower friends are forever friends!

And if this concludes the experience of these Daisies for the year, engage the girls in thinking about how they will participate in Girl Scouts next year. A new journey? A first camping adventure? Other events going on through your Girl Scout council? Be sure the girls (and their Friends and Family Network!) know how to keep their Girl Scout adventures growing!

To really get the girls thinking about what's possible as they grow up in Girl Scouts, invite them to check out the profile of Sohini Bandy on page 36 of their book. Sohini is a Girl Scout Gold Award winner from Austin, Texas, who, as a high school student, helped clear out vinca plants that were crowding a big stream called the Spicewood Tributary. Ask the girls to imagine the Girl Scout adventures they might enjoy when they are in high school!

NOW, TAKE SOME TIME FOR YOURSELF!

Now that you have guided girls along this journey *Between Earth and Sky*,
take a quiet moment to enjoy all you've accomplished.

What road will you travel next? Think about that as you ask yourself, so what have
I learned about leadership and me?

_____

_____

This journey led me to **DISCOVER** that I

_____

_____

By guiding girls to **CONNECT** with one another, I

_____

_____

Coaching girls to **TAKE ACTION** for the good of Earth taught me

_____

_____